Backcountry Skiing

California's High Sierra

John Moynier

FALCON®

HELENA, MONTANA

*A*FALCONGUIDE®

Falcon® Publishing is continually expanding its list of recreational guide-books. All books include detailed descriptions, accurate maps, and all information necessary for enjoyable trips. You can order extra copies of this book and get information and prices for other Falcon books by writing Falcon, P.O. Box 1718, Helena, MT 59624 or calling toll free 1-800-582-2665. Also, please ask for a free copy of our current catalog. Visit our website at www.FalconOutdoors.com or contact us by e-mail at falcon@falcon.com.

Library of Congress Cataloging-in-Publication Data

Moynier, John.
    Backbountry skiing in California's High Sierra / by John Moynier.
        p.   cm.
    Rev. ed. of: Backcountry Skiing in the High Sierra. c1992.
    Includes index.
    ISBN 1-56044-913-6 (pbk.)
    1. Cross-country skiing—Sierra Nevada (Calif. and Nev.) Guidebooks.
    2. Skis and skiing—Sierra Nevada (Calif. and Nev.)   3. Sierra Nevada
    (Calif. and Nev.) Guidebooks.
I. Moynier, John. Backcountry skiing in the High Sierra.   II. Title.
GV854.5.S5M69   1999   99-27439
917.94'40453—dc21   CIP

CAUTION

Outdoor recreational activities are by their very nature potentially hazardous. All participants in such activities must assume responsibility for their own actions and safety. The information contained in this guidebook cannot replace sound judgment and good decision-making skills, which help reduce risk exposure, nor does the scope of this book allow for disclosure of all the potential hazards and risks involved in such activities.

Learn as much as possible about the outdoor recreational activities in which you participate, prepare for the unexpected, and be cautious. The reward will be a safer and more enjoyable experience.

 Text pages printed on recycled paper.

WARNING
Backcountry skiing is a sport where you may be seriously injured or die. Read this before you use this book.

This guidebook is a compilation of unverified information gathered from many different sources. The author cannot assure the accuracy of any of the information in this book, including the topographic maps, the route descriptions, and the difficulty ratings. These may be incorrect or misleading. Also, ratings of difficulty and danger are always subjective and depend on the experience, technical ability, confidence, and physical fitness of the skier who supplied the rating. Therefore, be warned that you must exercise your own judgement on where a route goes, its difficulty, and your ability to safely protect yourself from the risks of ski mountaineering. Examples of some of these risks include: avalanches, falling due to technical difficulty or natural hazards, your own equipment failure, and failure or absence of fixed protection.

You should not depend on any information gleaned from this book for your personal safety; your safety depends on your own good judgement, based on experience and a realistic assessment of your climbing and skiing ability. If you have any doubt as to your ability to safely ski or descend a route described in this book, do not attempt it.

The following are some ways to make your use of this book safer:

1. Consultation: You should always consult with other skiers about the difficulty and danger of a particular route or descent prior to attempting it. Most locals are glad to give advice on routes in their area. We suggest that you contact locals to confirm ratings and safety of particular routes and to obtain firsthand information about a route chosen from this book.

2. Instruction: Most areas have local ski instructors and mountain guides. We recommend that you engage an instructor or guide to learn safety techniques and to become familiar with the routes and hazards of the areas described in this book. Even after you are proficient at backcountry touring and skiing descents safely, occasional use of a guide is a safe way to raise your skiing standard and learn advanced techniques.

Be aware of the following specific potential hazards that could arise in using this book:

1. Misdescriptions of Routes/Descents: If you climb or descend a route and you have a doubt as to where the route may go, you should not proceed unless you are sure that you can go that way safely. Route descriptions and topos in this book may be inaccurate or misleading.

2. Incorrect Difficulty Rating: A route may, in fact, be more difficult than the rating indicates. Do not be lulled into a false sense of security by the difficulty rating.

There are no warranties, whether express or implied, that this guidebook is accurate or that the information contained in it is reliable. There are no warranties of fitness for a particular purpose or that this guide is merchantable. Your use of this book indicates your assumption of the risk that it may contain errors and is an acknowledgment of your own sole responsibility for your climbing and skiing safety.

Acknowledgments

This book has been a community effort from day one, and as such, I would like to thank everyone who has provided me with information, helpful criticism, and inspiration over the past ten years. I would also like to thank all of those people who have accompanied me on these tours and descents. I am especially grateful for their patience and understanding, as time and again I would request first tracks under the pretext that I needed to get in a position to take photos.

I would particularly like to thank David Beck of Sierra Ski Touring for introducing me to backcountry skiing and serving as a mentor in my early guiding years. The same goes for Norm Wilson, who was a tremendous inspiration in terms of pursuing a lifelong love of the Sierra backcountry, as well as a patient teacher, sharing with me most of what I know about avalanche awareness. I owe a huge debt to Tom Carter, Chris Cox, Kimberly Walker, and especially the late Allan Bard for letting me tag along on trips with Alpine Expeditions. I not only learned a lot about skiing and guiding from Bardini and crew, but I also learned how to "red line the fun meter." I would also like to thank Doug Robinson, Galen Rowell, Dion Goldsworthy, and all of the folks that I met and worked with over the years at Rock Creek Winter Lodge for their inspiration, friendship, and shared turns.

In addition, I would like to thank the many people who graciously provided me with their extensive route knowledge and editorial assistance, as well as their excellent photographs. In particular, I would like to thank the following people for their extraordinary assistance in the development of this book: Craig Albright, Dave Braun, Vern Clevenger, John Dittli, Craig Dostie, Chris Falkenstein, Claude Fiddler, Tim Forsell, Richard Leversee, Chris Libby, Peter Mayfield, Andrew McLean, Tim Messick, George Meyers, Mark Nadell, Dennis Oakeshott, Dave Page, Paul Parker, Stephen Pope, Jim Stimson, Bela and Mimi Vadasz, and James Wilson. I could go on and on; there are literally hundreds of others who have helped. Thank you.

Finally, I would like to thank my wife, Rose, and daughter, Katie, for their wonderful love, patience, and inspiration. I couldn't do it without them.

Contents

Preface

When I began working on the first edition of this book almost a decade ago, the sport of backcountry skiing was quite different than it is now. Our focus then was on long tours and classic descents. The big deal was skiing the High Route or a section of the Redline Crest tour, maybe bagging Elderberry Canyon or cheating death in the Bloody Couloir. Nowadays, these things are commonplace and the cutting edge is a heck of a lot sharper. We can always claim that the gear held us back, but whatever the reason, the sport has changed.

This new edition reflects that change. When I first got into backcountry skiing in the late 1970s, Fischer 77s and Alfa Seniors were the hot ticket. Given enough slope, you could get these planks to turn (sort of). Wool knickers and sweaters were the uniform of choice, and alpaca hats from the Andes replaced balaclavas as the cool headgear. Five years later, Karhu Comps and Asolo Extremes felt like cheating. The debate was about double camber versus single camber and the invasion of plastic stiffeners into our leather boots. Sporty white caps replaced the fuzz head look, and Lycra began to replace our woolen undies.

The next big debate came and went with the steamroller effect of pin bindings on alpine skis and plastic boots with buckles. Sondre Norheim was turning in his grave, but the evolution kept on rolling. Now woolen watch caps are fashion items, and helmets have become almost mandatory as folks launch off huge cornices into narrow, rock-lined couloirs. Don't even mention snowboards. Once the knuckle-draggers hit the scene, there went the neighborhood.

The thing that hasn't changed is the lure of the High Sierra. Even as the generations change, so does our perception of what constitutes ski terrain. If much of the focus is gone from tours and turned toward descents, well, that's cool (I mean, it's hard to top the Redline). That's why this edition has an expanded section on peak descents. Sure, a lot of these shots are pretty stiff, but they all are doable by today's standards (especially when you include snowboards).

Perhaps the biggest change since the last edition, though, was the passing of longtime guide, mentor, author, and raconteur Allan Bard. The sage of the Sierra, the Great Bardini. We miss him greatly and this book is dedicated to him. This was Bardini's backyard, what he called the Promised Land. Allan felt more at home on the terrain described in these pages than he did anywhere else, and it would be impossible to have written this book without his assistance. Allan was a great friend and the best ski partner you could ever have. I hope that the Spirit of Bardini lives on in the pages of this book and that the Range of Light inspires you as it has so many of us. So grab your boards and let's go skiing!

Foreword to the First Edition

SKIING ON THE EAST SIDE BY ALLAN BARD

The rosy light of dawn drenches the snow-cloaked peaks visible from my kitchen window. Fifteen miles away and ten thousand feet above me, the prevailing wind scours the southern slopes and quietly drifts its wind-borne harvest into the north-facing bowls. As always, the smell of hot black coffee, the crackle of the woodstove, and the rumor of new snow in the hills promises another memorable day of skiing in the backyard.

I love this magnificent place covered in a mantle of fresh snow. It is just possibly the most wonderfully unique mountain range in the world for us backcountry skiing types. Of course, if you ask anyone about California snow, they'll tell you about Sierra cement. That may be true for the Tahoe area, but not here on the east side. Something magical happens when storms climb towards the Sierra Crest; the higher they get, the drier they get. By the time the snow takes up its seasonal residence here in God's Country, it is some kind of fabulous fluff—deep, too. There is snow that is as good as "the greatest snow on earth" you've heard bragged of elsewhere, and there's lots of it.

Tom Carter and Allan Bard on top of Mount Whitney. CHRIS COX PHOTO

But even on this morning—crisp with winter—it's not powder that comes to mind when I think of skiing the High Sierra, but spring corn. Not that granular junk you find in the Rockies late in the season. No, this stuff is velvet in texture and creamy to ski—ego snow we call it. In my humble opinion, there's nothing finer than corn-snow skiing on a spring day, and the High Sierra is perhaps Mother Nature's finest corn snow factory. The peaks here offer a unique combination of high altitude at low latitude, along with a fat snowpack and an incredibly long season. Mix in those famous sunny California days and cool mountain nights, and you have the fixings for a perennial crop of perfect Sierra corn.

And talk about terrain; this is backcountry skiing as God intended it. Thousands of square miles of wilderness to live out our skiing dreams. When I first began to explore this wonderful range, I felt like a kid in a candy store. Having our pick of the best skiing on the planet, we'd often start giggling like idiots, thankful for our good fortune at having landed in such an incredible place. Soon I began gaining my livelihood by introducing others to the charms of the range, guiding them in words and deeds through the Sierra.

Times change. I get a good laugh now thinking about the gear and the techniques that we used in those prehistoric days: toothpicks for skis, boots like floppy bedroom slippers, wool knickers, and klister. Now we're running fat skis and plastic boots, composite this and synthetic that. What hasn't changed is that backcountry skiing here still seems like a well-guarded secret. It can't be as good as they say, can it? Well it is. Twenty years later, I still love this place and I love sharing it with others. Looking back over those years, I know that skiing the High Sierra has enriched my life beyond all expectations. May it do the same for you.

Introduction

This guide is designed to be an introduction to the almost endless possibilities for backcountry skiing in the High Sierra. In my opinion, the High Sierra is perhaps the finest place in the world to seek the challenges of backcountry skiing. The abundant snowfall, moderate weather, and inviting terrain make the range a perfect place to explore on skis. The blanket of snow not only makes travel easier and often more fun, it also removes all sign of summer use and allows us to believe we are perhaps the first folks to explore the area. With beautiful spring weather, it's easy to see why summer visitors have often referred to the Sierra as the "gentle wilderness."

However, winters here are very snowy, and it can be a very harsh environment at times. Heavy snowfalls and high avalanche danger combined with remote locations can make even the shortest tours or descents very serious expeditions. The season for backcountry skiing in the Sierra generally runs from early November to mid-July. Summer skiing can also be found on the high glaciers and permanent snowfields, especially those accessed from US Highway 395 on the eastern side. Winter ski mountaineering is justifiably popular, especially from high base lodges like Rock Creek Lodge and Tioga Pass Resort.

There are many high roads and trails that begin to open in the spring, providing easy access to the high country, especially on the eastern side. However, the only road that crosses the High Sierra is the Tioga Pass Road in Yosemite National Park, and this is usually closed from early November to mid-May. All of this country is protected as national park or national forest, so once you leave the trailhead, you're almost guaranteed a true wilderness experience. Note that wilderness permits are required for overnight stays on all of these tours. For more information, see the appendix.

Be aware that ski tours that reach the heart of the range should be considered self-sufficient mini-expeditions. There are no huts, no rangers, and no radios to help you or to intrude upon your wilderness experience. Even cell phones may have limited success. However, it's a great feeling to know that even in crowded California, you really can get away from it all.

The easiest way to get into backcountry skiing is to pick a day's hiking trip with which you are familiar and try it on skis. You may be surprised that even the most familiar landmarks can look very different with a mantle of snow. The next step is to try an overnight snow camping trip close to the car. This will help you sort out gear and the basics of winter camping. Now you are ready to try a longer tour. Again, it's best to pick a route with which you're familiar.

The route you take will be different over snow, and you may even decide to use different passes or alternate routes once you see what the snow conditions are like. Regardless of their route, those folks who do decide to venture into the High Sierra in the off-season will be greatly rewarded. The stunning beauty of the winter landscape, the absolute quiet, and the feeling of truly being in the wilderness are worth the difficulties of backcountry ski travel a thousand times over.

Peter Campbell cresting out on Mono Pass, Rock Creek.

How to Use This Guide

This guide has been organized in a manner designed to introduce you to the joys and challenges of backcountry skiing in the High Sierra. Following a brief historical overview of the sport as practiced in the Sierra, the introductory sections offer advice on subjects including avalanche awareness, snow camping, and equipment. This is followed by an introduction to the methodology used to rate these tours. This section is especially important in terms of identifying whether a tour is within or beyond your capabilities, skills, and comfort zone. Finally, there is a section on how to get to these areas, as well as some of the regulatory information involved with traveling in this pristine wilderness.

The majority of the book describes long tours into the heart of the range. The first section of tours details skiing the Sierra Crest from south to north. The Sierra Crest, the equivalent of skiing the John Muir Trail, is broken into seven tours between logical trailheads. These tours generally require anywhere from three days to a week to complete. The second section profiles four trans-Sierra tours. These high-commitment expeditions cross the range on the major east-west divides and include the famous Sierra High Route and the popular tour from Mammoth to Yosemite. The final section of tours includes eight shorter tours that offer less of a commitment, but still provide challenging skiing.

The last section of the book describes sixty of the finest ski descents along the Sierra Crest. Many of these descents offer 5,000 feet of vertical or more, ranging from merely steep to steeper than an elevator shaft. Most of the big peaks are on this list, as well as some lesser-known classics that may provide even higher-quality skiing than their more famous neighbors. These peaks are listed from south to north, beginning with fourteeners like Mount Langley, Mount Whitney, Mount Williamson, and Mount Tyndall. This challenging list visits the summits of most of the highly sought-after peaks in the range. Just climbing these peaks is quite an accomplishment, let alone leaving tracks down their faces and hidden couloirs. Many of these descents are quite difficult, but overall, there is something for everyone.

History

We are soulless if we don't gain a sense of history and develop a respect for the pioneers of our sport. There has been a steady progression of backcountry skiing pioneers in the Sierra over the past 100 years, beginning with Snowshoe Thompson and his contemporaries. We can't help but respect the accomplishments of men such as Otto Steiner, who were making impressive ski descents and very fast traverses of routes like the High Route in the 1920s and 1930s. Snow surveyors like Orland Bartholomew were also exploring the Sierra. In 1929, Bartholomew made an incredible solo traverse of the Sierra Crest, basically following the John Muir Trail.

Mammoth Mountain pioneer and snow surveyor Dave McCoy and his friends were skiing the peaks of the eastern Sierra in the early 1930s. For many years they held a notable race down from the summit of Carson Peak. The winning times were often around five minutes for the 3,000-foot ungroomed run. The Sierra Club Ski Mountaineers have been active in the Sierra high country since the Great Depression, and well-known climbers like Norman Clyde and David Brower were very keen skiers. In fact, the bulk of the Sierra Club's definitive *Manual of Ski Mountaineering* was written on prewar trips to Clyde's base camp below Bear Creek Spire.

In the late 1960s, the local climbing community began exploring the backcountry. Galen Rowell, Doug Robinson, and John Fischer were among the most prominent activists. Bishop, California locals like Smoke Blanchard,

Orland Bartholomew skiing the John Muir Trail. PHOTO COURTESY OF DOUG ROBINSON

Tom Ross, Gordon Wiltsie, and Jay Jensen often accompanied them. They were joined by many excellent skiers from the Tahoe area, including Norm Wilson, H.J. Burhenne, David Beck, and Walt Herbert. In 1970, Dave McCoy's son Carl joined Doug Robinson to make the second ski traverse of the John Muir Trail on alpine touring equipment. In 1976, Beck and his wife Susan made the third traverse of the John Muir Trail on lightweight cross-country skis. The previous year, the Becks had joined forces with Nick Hartzell to pioneer the modern High Route.

In the 1970s and early 1980s, Yosemite Valley refugees like Dale and Allan Bard, Walter Rosenthal, Bob Locke, Chris Falkenstein, Tom Carter, Dennis Oakeshott, Werner Braun, Dan Conners, and Jim Stimson (and others) continued the tradition and pushed the extreme limits of the east side of the Sierra Crest, mostly on the primitive telemark equipment of the day. Some of their most impressive descents included *The Parachute* on Pyramid Peak, *The Cocaine Chute* on Dana Plateau, *The Scheelite Chute* on Wheeler Crest, and *The Solstice Couloir* on Mount Dana, as well as many short, steep shots like *The Ellery Chutes* and *The Rock Chute* on Sherwin Bowls.

In 1980, Doug Robinson enticed Colorado extreme skier Chris Landry to visit the Sierra after their impressive first ski descent of Liberty Ridge on Mount Rainier. Landry proceeded to blow everyone away with his descents of such classic Sierra ice climbs as the north face of Mount Darwin and *Right Mendel Couloir*. Landry is perhaps best remembered for his out-of-context, yet to-the-point, definition of extreme skiing—"If you fall, you die." His descent of *Mendel Couloir* was not repeated for almost 20 years.

Many other impressive events occurred over the next few years, culminating in the ultimate Sierra Crest tour known as The Redline. Taking parts of the 1983 and 1984 spring seasons, Tom Carter, Allan Bard, and Chris Cox skied the very crest of the range from Mount Langley in the south to Mammoth Mountain in the north. Climbing and then skiing each peak along the crest, their team made over 20 first descents in the process, including the north face of Mount Whitney, the north face of Mount Russell, and the northeast couloir of Mount Humphreys.

At this time, backcountry skiing in the Sierra really began to come to the forefront of the ski community's consciousness, with numerous articles appearing in national magazines, as well as various traveling slide shows and clinics presented by the local guiding community. Rock Creek Winter Lodge became a focal point for the eastern Sierra backcountry community with a well-stocked hut system, guided backcountry tours, and its infamous parties and sock hops.

By the late 1980s, a number of Southern California and Bay Area ski mountaineers had joined the locals in making first descents up and down the range. During the 1980s, there was also a push to ski long tours very quickly on lightweight gear. Examples included a couple of Colorado Outward Bound instructors skiing the John Muir Trail in seven days, and Doug Robinson skiing the High Route in less than 24 hours. Tours like Mammoth to Yosemite, Rock Creek to Mammoth, and Piute Pass to Rock Creek were frequently skied as day tours, and some skiers like Marty Hornick even went against the clock on these sections, continually lowering their times. This trend goes on today as veterans of the Tahoe race scene, like Mark Nadell, Peter Mayfield, and Jeff Schloss, blitz sections of the crest on skating gear.

In the early 1990s, Dave McCoy's grandsons Davey and Ronny pioneered ever-steeper lines on skis and snowboards. Along with their fellow extreme friends, like Glen Plake, Jason Moore, and Steve Klassen, they've picked off many of the remaining skiable lines on the crest, including the central couloir on Split Mountain, *Mendenhall Couloir* on Laurel Mountain, the north couloir of Mount Emerson, *Checkered Demon Couloir* on Peak 13,112, and *Death Couloir* on Mount Morrison.

Traveling extreme skiers and snowboarders like Jim and Bonnie Zellers, Andrew McLean, and David Braun have also made many impressive descents recently including the north couloir on Feather Peak, the second descent of *Mendel Couloir*, the north face of Mount Williamson and *Zebra Couloir* on Mount Emerson. What does the future hold in the new millennium? Only time will tell, but it will certainly be exciting.

HIGH SIERRA WEATHER

Weather in the High Sierra, like any major mountain range, is often unpredictable. Winters here are generally typified by long periods of wonderfully clear weather interspersed with intense storms that can last a week or more. These patterns are dictated primarily by the northern path of the winter jet stream and the presence (or absence) of the Great Basin High, a regional cell of high pressure that often sets up over southern Utah. Normal winter daytime temperatures at 10,000 feet are in the teens or low 20s, while nighttime lows are generally around zero (Fahrenheit). Spring is warmer, with highs in the 40s and lows in the teens or low 20s.

The High Sierra is generally a windy place, and ridgetop winds of 60 miles per hour or more are not uncommon. The prevailing winds come from the southwest and drive the standard storm pattern. Winter storms generally originate in the Gulf of Alaska and often bring snowfalls of two to three feet or more.

At least once a year, a major Pacific storm system will hit the area, resulting in what is affectionately known as the Pineapple Connection. This occurs when a cold, low-pressure air mass from the Gulf of Alaska collides with a warm, subtropical high south of Hawaii. This creates a turnstile effect that accelerates the midwinter jet stream and slams the storm into central California with astonishing fury. When these conditions are forecasted, it's best to postpone your touring plans and enjoy the fine deep snow skiing at the lift-served areas. A prime example of this occurred in February 1986 when over 14 feet of snow fell in one week; another occurred in February 1998 when it snowed 24 out of 28 days and dumped more than 20 feet.

As these storms move east, they often stall out in central Nevada, creating a condition known as a Tonopah Low. When this happens, the winds shift to the northeast, bringing very cold temperatures and light to moderate snowfall. The upslope nature of these winds also frequently strips much of the new snow from loaded areas, ruining the powder skiing except in protected areas. It is rare for cold northern storms to reach this far south, but when they do, bitterly cold temperatures and strong north winds may linger for a week or more.

Occasionally, we'll get a period where the jet stream sets its sights directly on the High Sierra and storms stack up across the Pacific to Japan. It may snow for weeks straight, and this is no time to be in the backcountry. During El Niño conditions, this pattern can continue for most of the winter, as it did in 1969, 1978, 1982, 1983, 1986, 1993, 1995, and 1998. In these years, we may get over 50 feet of snow at the upper elevations in a season that lasts from October into July or August. Of course, the flip side of this is that we sometimes get hit by drought conditions and the weather can be very nice (and dry) for weeks on end. The fickle nature of our winter weather is a good reason why it's usually best to wait until spring to try more adventurous tours or descents.

A typical winter? Generally, our winters begin with a couple of decent snowfalls in late September or October. These early storms can be very cold and may last a week or more. Unfortunately, this often means that the very base of the snowpack may eventually consist of rotten, faceted grains later in the year. Thanksgiving is traditionally the beginning of our season and is often a stormy time, as is the Christmas break. Generally, we can count on a solid base and excellent skiing by New Year's Eve. After the New Year, there often seems to be a period when a high-pressure system settles over the region and we get a couple of weeks of cold, stable weather. This can be a good time to head into the backcountry, provided you don't mind long, frigid nights and short, chilly days. February through early March is historically the worst time to venture in the backcountry because this is when we often get our biggest storms. During late March and into early April, the weather can either be very stormy or really beautiful. Long tours in these months must be planned with an eye for long-term weather forecasts.

Most folks plan their long tours for late spring when the weather is more stable and the snowpack has settled. Mid-April to mid-June is the best time to enjoy the Sierra. In spring, freezing temperatures at night and warm temperatures during the day work to create the corn snow for which the Sierra is justly famous. This mature melt-freeze snow resembles glacial névé and provides an ideal surface for skiing. However, there always seems to be a period in early April (known as the spring thaw) when daytime temperatures are high and nighttime temperatures fail to drop below freezing. When this happens, the snow can rot quickly and we may experience big avalanches on all aspects and at all times of the day.

We are really fortunate to enjoy such a long ski season in the Sierra. About the time when folks in Colorado or Utah are hanging up their skis and hopping onto their mountain bikes, the skiing here is just starting to get good. Mammoth Mountain Ski Area has often been open for skiing through the Fourth of July, and in many years the backcountry skiing has stayed good throughout the summer. That's why a lot of us never put our skis away for the season—there are always a few turns to be had on the small glaciers and permanent snowfields hidden along the crest.

AVALANCHE AWARENESS

Many backcountry travelers choose to believe that there is no such thing as avalanche hazard, but this is either through ignorance or foolishness. Some people may not want to let negative thoughts intrude on their ski fun, while others who've had experience in other ranges may be blind to the dangers here. Many are just not educated about the dangers of avalanches. However, there is definitely a real threat of avalanches here, demanding attention and concern, whether in the Sierra, Wasatch, or Rockies.

Here's the scoop: Anyone traveling in the backcountry needs to recognize the risks involved with backcountry skiing, and concern for avalanche hazard should be first and foremost in the mind of anyone who attempts a tour or descent in steep terrain. Although some areas may be more consistently hazardous than others, there will likely be serious avalanche hazard at certain times in certain seasons at some point on all of these tours and peaks. This doesn't mean that you will always be at risk, but you must have a strong enough background in evaluating snow conditions to know when hazard exists, as well as when it is reasonable to enjoy these adventures safely.

This short introduction to avalanche awareness is just that, an introduction. Learn all you can by reading books and taking avalanche field courses that focus on hazard evaluation and self-rescue techniques. It is the responsibility of each member of a group to evaluate his or her own risk when traveling through this terrain. Avalanche awareness is developed through education, as well as practical experience and observation. Without a well-developed sense of hazard awareness, you are playing avalanche roulette every time you head into the winter backcountry. Sooner or later, the odds are going to stack up against you.

Most backcountry skiers will eventually find themselves exposed to some avalanche hazard. In fact, most of the slopes we enjoy skiing can be classified as prime avalanche terrain. In a sense, ignorance is bliss. As you learn more about hazard evaluation, you'll probably recall numerous instances when you were at more risk than you realized. However, you can't always count on luck. An hour earlier or later, or a hundred feet to one side or the other, you might have become a statistic.

Spring avalanche on Sawtooth Ridge.

11

The first step to skiing the backcountry safely is learning how to recognize avalanche terrain. Along with this, we must learn to recognize the conditions that make this terrain dangerous. The next step is acknowledging that weather and snowpack conditions can change quickly with time; so, you must learn to read how these changes affect the stability of the snowpack. Finally, you must know what to do when everything comes unglued despite your best efforts, and the hills start coming down around your ears.

Judgment, knowledge, and experience must become your guides. Form an opinion about stability before you even leave the trailhead, and be prepared to change your opinion as conditions change. Gather all the information you can before your trip by calling the National Weather Service or by accessing its website on the Internet. Get a local avalanche forecast if one is available, or call someone in the area to obtain local observations. You can also check out the local forecast on the Internet at www.csac.brg.

Keep your eyes and mind open as you travel. Nature generally provides obvious clues to stability if you know how and where to look. Listen to the snow, feel it with your poles and skis, and constantly evaluate each step or turn. Be prepared to augment or even completely overhaul your assessment along the way. Make sure everyone in your group carries a beacon, shovel, and probes and knows how to use them. Finally, don't be too stubborn to leave the slope for another day. Below are a few things to keep in mind for safely enjoying avalanche terrain.

Slope angle. When planning a trip or picking a route, remember that slope angles of 30 to 50 degrees (advanced to expert alpine runs at a ski area) are the most likely to slide, especially convex slopes, which are under more internal tension. Avalanche statistics show that slopes of 38 degrees are prime avalanche terrain. Note that even low-angled slopes can be threatened by steeper slopes above. Steeper slopes generally slough off new snow before they build up significant accumulations, but really wet snow can stick to very steep slopes, especially when deposited by strong winds.

Aspect. Slope aspect is a prime factor in determining avalanche hazard. Sunny south aspects are most likely to slide right after a storm as a result of rapid warming, but they are also are quickest to stabilize due to the warmer temperatures. Shady north slopes are less likely to be affected by the sun, but they are also more likely to harbor or encourage the development of weak layers over long periods of cold, dry weather, especially early in the season. Orientation to the wind is even more critical. Windward slopes are likely to be scoured during storms, while dangerous slabs are frequently deposited on lee slopes.

Cornices. The wind can also form extremely large cornices on ridgetops. These features can be very unstable and may threaten more moderate slopes below. When skiing along a ridge, always stay much farther back from the edge than appears necessary because cornices may bridge nonobvious gaps in the crest. The soft, pillowy area just below a cornice is often a slab, deposited by the eddying effect of the wind. These cohesive layers can release catastrophically with the additional weight of a skier or if the cornice breaks and falls on them.

Routefinding. Once in the backcountry, it's important to pick a route that avoids primary avalanche terrain if at all possible, because conditions may change from day to day or hour to hour. When in doubt, pick a route that follows a ridgetop or wide valley bottom if possible. Look for signs of previous avalanche activity, such as vegetation cues, old fracture lines, and debris piles, and avoid them. Stay clear of likely slide paths and runout zones, too, if at all possible. Densely timbered slopes are generally safer than open slopes, but they don't necessarily mean safety. If you can comfortably ski through the trees, an avalanche can definitely slide through them.

Recent avalanche activity. Once you learn to recognize avalanche terrain, the next step is to recognize whether it will stay put while you're there. The most important clue to snow stability is signs of recent avalanches on slopes of similar aspect and slope angle. Fresh fractures, blocks of debris, and large sunballs must not be ignored. These are very important clues that snow conditions are unstable. Rapid settling of the snow from tree branches or exposed cliffs should be considered a potential sign of instability.

Weather. It's important to note that weather events are key to developing avalanche hazard. Most slides occur either during or immediately after a storm or wind-loading event. New deposition of an inch an hour or 2 feet in 24 hours should be a warning sign. Double this and you've got serious problems in steep terrain. Note that even moderate winds can increase the hazard by transporting snow from one area to another, often depositing dangerous slabs on lee slopes in a short period of time. Other weather factors that warrant concern include rain, fog, or warm wind.

Temperature and humidity. High relative humidity can cause rimming of snow crystals or create a slick layer on the snow, which could become a dangerous slide surface given enough time. Temperatures well above or below freezing can also lead to decreased stability of the snowpack, as can any sudden change in temperature. These factors affect the relative density of surface layers, as well as the bonding of the crystals within a given layer of the snowpack.

Snowpack layers. The snowpack itself is also of primary interest. Layers of snow within the pack can act cohesively as slabs. Poor bonding between layers is a common cause of avalanches because the overlying layers cut loose in shear failure on the contact surface. Density incongruities should also be noted. Denser layers overlying less dense layers are always a concern. Other potentially weak areas include buried ice crusts or thin, weak layers of poorly bonded snow like buried surface hoar or old, faceted crystals.

Snowpack stability. The processes that lead to increased or decreased stability are also important. A deep snowpack and moderate temperatures will lead to a small temperature gradient through the pack. The physics of this leads to greater snowpack stability through a process that results in a net decrease in crystal size and a net increase in the bonding strength between the crystals. Shallow snowpacks and/or very cold temperatures can lead to significant temperature differences between the ground and the surface. These conditions tend to rot the snow from the ground up toward the surface by destroying the bonds between the crystals as the crystals themselves grow. This can also happen higher in a snowpack, especially on cool, clear nights.

Alternating very warm days and cold nights can lead to a very strong snowpack, bonded by a melt-freeze process. As the snowpack cools at night, free water in the snowpack refreezes to glue the crystals together. All of the above processes might occur in the same snowpack. You can check on the snow conditions below the surface by digging a pit in the snow or probing with your ski pole. If you are still unsure about a slope, you should perform a shovel shear or Rutschblock ski test to determine stability.

Communication. Always make sure that everyone understands and approves of the group's objectives and that alternate routes have been considered. Listen to your intuition. If your gut tells you things are amiss, the time to act is now. Don't let the idea "I don't want to spoil it for the group" lead to tragedy. Stand up for your opinion and don't worry about being a party pooper. It is much better to err on the safe side and come back another day than to have to dig a buddy out of a pile of debris. Communicate your plans constantly and make sure everyone understands.

Equipment. Avalanche transceivers or beacons have proven to be the most effective method of finding someone who has been completely buried in a slide. If your partners follow good protocol and have practiced search techniques, then they should be able to find you within a short period of time. That doesn't mean that you will still be alive, however, but at least you have a much better chance of surviving than without a beacon. In order to dig through heavy avalanche debris, each person will also need a sturdy shovel. A set of probe poles will also make the efforts of rescuers more efficient because they can pinpoint your location without wasting effort digging a foot or two to the side. Remember: Time is critical.

Hazardous areas. If you must travel in a hazardous area, limit your exposure. Travel one at a time, with beacons on transmit, and all eyes on the person crossing. Take advantage of safer areas like dense timber, rock outcrops, ridges, and wide valley bottoms. If you must cross a suspect slope, do so as high as possible, preferably on the ridgetop. If you must ascend or descend a dangerous slope, stay close to the edge and choose as vertical a line as possible. Kicking steps straight up or down is much safer than cutting the slope with traverses, turns, or sitzmarks. Don't assume a slope is safe just because someone else has skied it, and remember that traveling on a low-angled slope can trigger steeper slopes above or sympathetically release a slope some distance away under really hazardous conditions.

Caution. Finally, the best overall strategy is to use caution and be prepared. As noted above, make sure everyone has a functioning avalanche transceiver and knows how to use it. These should be turned on to transmit at the start of the day, checked, and left on until everyone is safely in camp. And don't forget, each person should also have a sturdy shovel and avalanche probe poles. The ski area maxim "Be aware, ski with care" is the absolute law of the backcountry. Travel one at a time in suspect areas, and always pick the safest route possible unless you are absolutely sure of a slope and snowpack stability. Backcountry skiing can be a very safe and rewarding experience if everyone accepts these responsibilities.

BACKCOUNTRY TRAVEL

Safe travel in the wintry Sierra depends on a number of skills. The most obvious are skiing skills, but it is far more valuable to have a well-developed sense of avalanche hazard awareness (discussed above) and strong mountain skills. Along with these come basic mountaineering skills such as using an ice axe and crampons, as well as basic rope handling. It is also important to have a knowledge of routefinding and wilderness first aid.

Ski mountaineering. Some of the trips listed in this book fall into the realm of ski mountaineering and require care on both the climb and the descent. Most of the passes on these tours are steep enough that you may feel more comfortable using an ice axe for a self-belay instead of skis or poles. When faced with firm spring snow, hard windboard, or frozen spring conditions, crampons will definitely save time and energy that might be otherwise spent kicking steps or desperately chopping toeholds.

Due to the pitch of many of the descents, as well as the exposure of some of the passes, you may occasionally want a hand line or even a belay. It's also quite possible that you may need to rappel off a cornice or a short stretch of cliff. On a tour in a low snow year, you may encounter more off-ski climbing, but monster cornices can be equally challenging in bigger snow years. That is why rope-handling skills can be very useful.

The same care and caution should be used when traveling over the loose rock found in some areas. In addition, I should also mention dicey creek and lake crossings. It's always worth looking for a solid snowbridge before attempting to cross a stream, especially if you can see or hear running water. As far as trusting lake ice, you must use your own judgement. The ice is generally weakest at the inlet and outlet, but there are often hidden thin spots or even open water in the middles of lakes. There have been a number of cases of backcountry skiers breaking through the ice of lakes and drowning because their packs and skis weighted them down. If you must cross, undo your pack's waist belt so you can escape if you get dunked.

Skiing skills. In terms of skiing or riding ability, it may not seem heroic, but just being solid on sideslipping and traverses is more important than being able to do jump telemarks in the bumps or crank squiggles in powder. These backcountry routes require much more than the ability to rip the fall line at the local ski hill. Out here, you need to ski well within your ability because there is no such thing as a pro ski patrol on the Sierra Crest. The backcountry is no place to practice your turns, especially with a heavy pack. Balancing under the weight of your pack while sliding on these skinny little sticks is plenty challenging without trying to pull off a move you're not sure you can make with your ACL intact.

When in doubt, downclimb or sideslip steep sections. Although it may seem odd, you can leave your skins on for descents. It's certainly safer to slowly glide down from a pass on skins than to careen out of control through suncups or sharp rocks at Mach two or perform repeated noseplows and have to pick yourself (and your pack) off the snow over and over. Remember, a broken leg or dislocated shoulder can be very serious far from the car, and you must be entirely self-sufficient and capable of effecting any self-rescue necessary when you undertake these trips.

A note about snowboards. Safe travel in the wintry Sierra on a snowboard requires special considerations. There's no better tool for the backcountry when the route is straightforward, but snowboards can be a real pain when things get interesting. The trips listed in this book fall into the realm of ski mountaineering and require care on both the climb and the descent. Proper trip planning will tell you whether snowboards are viable tools or whether you should opt for skis. Although particularly well-suited for descents in all kinds of snow conditions, snowboards in general are not particularly well-suited for touring. Aside from the recent offering of split boards, getting your board to the top of a peak can take a lot of the fun out of the whole experience.

Navigational skills. Equally important are good routefinding and navigational skills. You must be able to navigate by map and compass and understand the significance of features on a topographic map. An altimeter is also valuable to augment your map and compass, especially in whiteout or blizzard conditions. Choosing the wrong drainage or pass can be exhausting at best and disastrous at worst. The snowy Sierra can be a disorienting place and many experienced mountaineers have gotten very lost (and embarrassed) on these tours. In particular, Lamarck Col, The Tablelands, Tyndall Plateau, and Humphreys Basin are classic places to lose your way. The tragic experience of the Donner Party should not be lost on us.

Learning to navigate by landmarks in open country comes with practice, but picking the easiest route through cliffs, broken terrain, or a dense forest takes much more skill. That's why some of the route descriptions are purposefully vague; depending on snow conditions in a particular year, the route you take may be significantly different from the one I've described. Conditions constantly change, and a shift in the wind could put an impassable cornice over what usually is a relatively easy pass. As a result, you really need to be able to assess things for yourself when it comes to the exact route you take on these tours.

First aid. As long as I'm preaching caution and self-sufficiency, I will continue by encouraging everyone in a party to have a basic understanding of mountaineering first aid and the ability to deal with the most common problems like blisters, frostbite, hypothermia, and altitude sickness. Someone in the party should also have enough experience to recognize the symptoms of pulmonary or cerebral edema. The group's first aid kit should be able to handle anything from a bad sunburn to snow blindness or a broken femur, as well as contain the necessary tools for making an emergency sled to transport an injured member of your party. These days, a cellular phone is an essential first aid item.

SNOW CAMPING

I mentioned that most of these tours are like backpacking on snow. However, that "on snow" part does lead to some interesting peculiarities. For instance, unless you really like to waste hours melting snow for water, camping near a water source can be very important. With an ice axe or strong shovel, you can generally break through the ice of a lake or stream to get water, but remember that you still have to treat the water for parasites (like *Giardia*), just as in summer.

The location of your campsite is generally more important in winter than in summer. It might seem that camping under a tree would provide more shelter, but in the winter this can be deadly. Heavily weighted branches and snow bombs can drop at any time, easily crushing you and your tent. In addition, beware of exposed campsites at the foot of a pass or ridge that might be in a runout zone for rockfalls, avalanches, or cornice releases.

Exposure to wind is also a major concern. In addition to the chilling properties of a stiff breeze, Sierra winds can pick up a tent (even with you and your buddies in it) and roll it a long way. Camps with flat rocks or sand will allow you to stay drier and spread yourselves and your gear out to dry— it's especially important to dry out your sleeping bag. When sleeping on snow, you'll need to pack down a tent platform with your skis or feet. Building shallow walls around it will help anchor the tent in a storm. If you are going to be making a base camp, it's worth bringing along extra anchors so you don't need to use your skis.

There are some other important strategies for picking a winter camp. Remember that cold winds blow down-canyon at night and that light early

High camp below Picture Peak on the Evolution Loop. TIM FORSELL PHOTO

in the morning is often more desirable than light late in the evening. Lightning isn't as great a concern on winter trips, but you'll still want to keep it in mind when placing a camp in a storm. Flat meadows or frozen lakes may seem like inviting sites, yet they're notorious traps for cold air, and moving your camp a few feet upslope can make a big difference. Placing a camp in the shadow of a big peak will definitely make it hard to get out of your bag and into frozen boots in the morning. Plan your camps so that if a storm comes in, you won't be trapped on the wrong side of a pass or in a hazardous location. You may also want to choose a site so that you can get over a pass early in the morning while the avalanche hazard is lower or later in the day when an icy surface has softened.

It's often worth the extra effort to dig out a separate kitchen with a tarp overhead and to carve out benches to sit on. It's especially important to rig some kind of latrine so you don't just dump your dirty dishwater out in the snow and melt it again for your breakfast coffee. The same goes for toilet technique. Rather than pooping randomly in the snow, use rocket boxes or plastic buckets lined with plastic trash bags, and pack the containers out to a decent disposal site. On a tour, you must find a boulder field or an area that is far away from any water source or use area. A misplaced dump will melt through, toilet paper and all, to the water or ground below. Think of where you would go in the summer and use similar toilet etiquette. For more information, check out Will Harmon's informative book *Leave No Trace* (Falcon Publishing).

EQUIPMENT

All of these tours and descents have been done with modern telemark or randonée gear, and many tours have been done with snowboards and snowshoes or alpine ski gear. No matter what your preference in terms of transportation, make sure your boots are comfortable and fit well before you start trudging any distance in them. Walking up a hill is very different from downhill skiing at a lift-served area, and bad blisters will ruin even the most spectacular tour or thrilling descent.

Skis. For skis, climbing skins are worth their weight in gold. In the Sierra, adhesive-backed, nylon skins are more popular than strap-on styles because they allow you to edge on hard snow. Synthetic skins provide decent glide while maintaining maximum uphill grip, and they dry out much faster. It's a good idea to touch up the glue before every trip, but duct tape can help if the glue starts to fail. Ski crampons can help, too. Telemark or randonée gear is preferable for covering ground on longer tours. Snowshoes, snowboards, or alpine skis work okay for short distances, but they're no fun at all in deep snow or after a couple of miles of flat touring.

Snowboards. As for snowboards, you must choose a board that is light enough to carry yet can handle a broad range of snow conditions. Most backcountry riders prefer a soft boot and strap-type binding system. They like the soft boots for comfort and the simplicity of the strap system. Step-in systems are growing in popularity and offer obvious advantages in certain conditions, including added safety in the event of an avalanche. However, there are still a number of mountain guides, climbers, and cross-over skiers who prefer hard boots and plate bindings. Hard boots perform much like typical alpine climbing boots, accepting crampons and offering excellent protection from wet and cold. Kicking steps is also easier with hard boots, and this can be critical on frosty morning ascents in spring.

Poles. Another consideration is the use of poles. Backcountry skiers and snowshoers would feel lost without their poles, especially on the ascent. Many snowboarders, however, have no interest in the use of poles. This may be shortsighted. Not only is it easier to climb with the help of poles, but they can be used for self-arrest in the event of a fall. Using poles on the descent also merits consideration. Poles allow you to push across short flat sections, saving you from the one-legged skate or worse. Poles can also help with balance at the end of a run, keeping you from sitting in the snow. Finally, poles can be a major help when getting up from a fall in deep snow.

Camping Gear. Internal frame packs are your best bet for longer tours, because they keep your center of gravity close to your body and improve balance. A warm sleeping bag and pad are essential, in addition to some other form of shelter. Four-season, freestanding tents are the most popular, although many folks prefer the pyramid-style tarps because they're versatile and lightweight. A good, hot-burning stove that is maintenance-free is a must—the hotter it is, the faster it will melt snow for water. Taking food that you like is as important as its weight and ease of preparation. You burn a lot more calories just staying warm in winter. Anyone for a second helping of tasteless gruel?

The equipment list for backcountry touring should include a light ice axe. If used for nothing else, it can stake your tent down while you're out skiing. Most folks will choose to take a 100-foot or longer coil of 7 or 8 mm rope on more difficult tours for the reasons stated earlier. Everyone in the group should have a functioning avalanche transceiver and a sturdy shovel and should know how to use them.

There should be a least one good first aid kit and repair kit in the group. The repair kit should include a pair of light vise-grips, duct tape, pole-splinting materials, spare baskets, 5-minute epoxy, and binding repair stuff, as well as a means

Bonnie Zellers riding the Checkered Demon.
RICHARD LEVERSEE PHOTO

of making a sled out of skis, shovels, and poles. Other equipment to add to the list: extra water bottles, toilet paper, a headlamp, spare lighters or matches, map and compass, knife, and really good sunglasses and sunscreen.

Clothing. There are so many good synthetic alternatives to down, wool, and cotton these days that I don't need to mention them. By now everyone's probably sick of hearing about the layering concept, too. Just remember that a down jacket over a T-shirt (or shorts over long underwear) doesn't really cut it. Choosing what to bring and wear is important. You want to wear just enough to keep from getting chilled, or you'll overheat while slogging over a pass. Yet, you want to have enough warm stuff with you to enjoy the evening light after dinner. Although we're not talking fashion and outdoor clothing is a matter of personal taste, I have some general recommendations.

A good warm hat, as well as a light sun hat, is very important. Weather pants and a parka make stormy days a lot nicer, as do a pair of good gloves or mittens and a neck gaiter or scarf. Bicycling gloves are very comfortable on sunny spring tours. Extra dry socks and a pair of camp booties are necessities. I feel the same way about packing a warm, dry set of clothes to sleep in—you'll really be a lot more comfortable. I like to bring a lightweight down or synthetic jacket for evening wear and then use it for a pillow. However, you still have to fit all this stuff into your comfortable, sleek touring pack and carry it. As with all equipment, you must balance the need to go fast and light with the desire to be self-sufficient and comfortable.

RATINGS

The tours in this book are rated using a variation of the traditional Sierra Club system; I have tweaked this system a bit to adopt it for ski mountaineering. Be aware that these ratings are very general, and snow conditions may cause these ratings to vary dramatically. Other rating systems exist elsewhere, but this one works for me.

Class 1: Flat terrain (less than 10 degrees) requiring basic skiing skills. There are no Class 1 tours included in this book. Marcus Libkind's *Ski Tours in the Sierra Nevada, Vol. I-IV*, published by Wilderness Press, is a good reference for easier tours.

Class 2: Rolling terrain (up to 25 degrees) requiring intermediate skiing skills, but no mountaineering skills. Recommended gear includes climbing skins.

Class 3: Involves steep terrain (up to 35 degrees) requiring advanced skiing skills and avalanche awareness. Necessary gear includes climbing skins, an ice axe, and an 8 mm rope to belay over short stretches if conditions warrant it.

Class 4: Involves very steep terrain (35 to 45 degrees) requiring expert skiing skills, as well as a thorough knowledge of advanced mountaineering skills, such as belaying, rappelling, and anchoring. Necessary gear includes climbing skins, an ice axe, an 8 mm rope, crampons, and a selection of long slings and chocks for anchoring belays.

Class 5: Extremely steep terrain (over 45 degrees) requiring a high degree of skill in all aspects of ski mountaineering. The consequences of a fall in

The author skiing down Pine Creek Canyon.
MICK HAMPTON PHOTO

this terrain almost certainly would be fatal. In Class 4 or 5 (or even 3) terrain, it's up to you to decide when to pull out the rope. Necessary equipment for a Class 5 descent includes everything needed for Class 4, plus a diverse rack of rock, ice, and snow anchors for belaying and rappelling.

The combination of ratings (for example, Class 2-3 or Class 3-4) reflect potential changes in conditions that could seriously affect the situation you may encounter. In the interest of safety, always be prepared for the worst and use these ratings only as a rough guide. Remember that icy or unconsolidated conditions always make things more hazardous, as does the presence of cornices or poorly bonded slabs.

Since the publication of the first edition of this book, I've had a few people take issue with the ratings listed for various tours. In many cases, I have revised ratings based on their input. However, no rating system is perfect. A different way to look at these ratings would be via the "pucker factor," as follows. Class 1 is casual (as in no sweat). Class 2 is interesting (as in steep enough to keep you on your toes). Class 3 is scary (as in it would not be pretty if you fell). Class 4 is very scary (as in there is a high mangle potential if you fell). Class 5 is suicide (as in a fall would be certain death). Therefore, a trip in this guide that is rated Class 4, like Monarch Divide or a descent of *Bloody Couloir,* is likely to be very scary, involving serious terrain and snow conditions that require solid mountaineering skills, as well as expert skiing skills.

As a final note, I have known many expert alpine skiers who were scared to death on the ascent, only to become very comfortable once they stepped into their bindings to descend the same slope. On the other hand, I have been with skilled climbers who were very comfortable climbing the steepest slopes unroped, only to become an accident waiting to happen when they pointed their skis downhill. Ratings are entirely subjective and a poor tool at best for representing the real world. Ultimately, you're on your own, and you will have to be honest about assessing conditions and your own abilities.

California High Sierra Locator Map

GETTING THERE

The crest of the Sierra Nevada runs from the northwest to the southeast, and access is generally best from the west or the east. The closest airports to this region are Fresno on the west side and Reno on the east side. There are small airports in Bishop and Mammoth Lakes, but currently no regular air service from areas other than Los Angeles, and this is expensive. Bus service to the Sierra exists, but it is not dependable or convenient. Overall, a car is really the only practical option to access these trips.

The Sierra is flanked by California 99 on the west and US Highway 395 on the east. To the north, all-season US Highway 50 and Interstate 80 cross the Sierra near Lake Tahoe. US Highway 6 gives access to the Owens Valley from the east, while California 14 connects US 395 to Los Angeles. In the winter, there are no open roads that cross the Sierra from Walker Pass in the south (near Lake Isabella) to Carson Pass in the north (near Lake Tahoe).

California 108 and CA 120 are the only roads that cross the High Sierra in summer. They offer convenient access when they are open. However, both of these roads are generally closed from November until Memorial Day. California 108 links Sonora and Bridgeport via Sonora Pass and provides access to some fine skiing in the bowls near the pass. California 120 links Yosemite Valley with the eastern Sierra via Tuolumne Meadows and Tioga Pass and provides access to the Yosemite high country. When these roads open in the spring, they provide great access to a wide variety of skiing opportunities. Just don't be disappointed if they are closed when you get there.

Many spur roads lead into various west-side trailheads from Fresno and CA 99. California 198 accesses Mineral King and Giant Forest from the south via the towns of Visalia and Three Rivers. California 180 reaches Kings Canyon and Sequoia National parks. California 168 leads east past Huntington Lake to trailheads at Lake Edison and Florence Lake. California 41 leads north through Oakhurst and reaches Yosemite Valley, the spur road to Glacier Point, and CA 120.

Bishop is located between Reno and Los Angeles on US 395 and serves as the hub for the southern end of the east Sierra. The town of Mammoth Lakes is an hour north of Bishop and serves the central portion of the east side—with all of the expected amenities of a ski resort town. The smaller towns of Lone Pine, Independence, Big Pine, June Lake, Lee Vining and Bridgeport lie on or near US 395 and offer basic amenities like grocery stores, motels, showers, and restaurants. For backpacking, climbing, and skiing supplies, as well as current condition reports, contact Wilson's Eastside Sports (760) 873-7520 in Bishop, Kittredge Sports (760) 934-7566 in Mammoth Lakes, or Alpenglow (916) 583-6917 in Tahoe City.

SOAPBOX

One disturbing trend that has arisen recently does need to be addressed and that is the use of snowmobiles to access the backcountry. This is not in itself a bad thing, although the tradition in the Sierra has long been to "earn your

Catching air above avalanche debris on Pointless Peak.

turns." The problem involves the use of motorized vehicles in the wilderness, which is illegal. This is not about leaving a track that will melt in spring; it's about noise, exhaust, and unseen impact to underlying sensitive plants, animals, and habitat.

Some of the most impressive descents done in recent years were snowmobile-assisted, often deep into the wilderness. I have no desire to condone these deeds, however noteworthy the descent. The law is very clear here and is designed to protect the wilderness environment.

Although I have nothing against snowmobiles or their use for backcountry access in legal areas, let's all work together to protect this precious resource—the wilderness—and leave the machines at the boundary. I know that sometimes the boundary line is arbitrary and unclear, but let's use common sense regarding mechanized access to this wonderful backcountry playground.

Sierra Crest Tours

Sierra Crest Tours

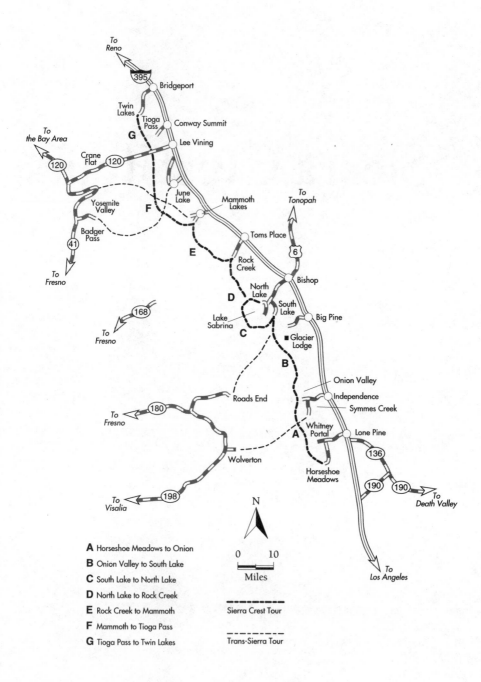

To Reno

395 Bridgeport

Twin Lakes

Tioga Pass

Conway Summit

To the Bay Area

G Lee Vining

Crane Flat

120 120

June Lake

Mammoth Lakes

To Tonopah

Yosemite Valley

F

Badger Pass

41

To Fresno

E

Toms Place

6

Rock Creek

168

D North Lake

South Lake

Bishop

To Fresno

Lake Sabrina

C

Big Pine

Glacier Lodge

B

Onion Valley

180

Roads End

Independence

Symmes Creek

To Fresno

A Whitney Portal

Lone Pine

Wolverton

136

198

Horseshoe Meadows

190 190

To Visalia

To Death Valley

N

0   10

Miles

A Horseshoe Meadows to Onion
B Onion Valley to South Lake
C South Lake to North Lake
D North Lake to Rock Creek
E Rock Creek to Mammoth
F Mammoth to Tioga Pass
G Tioga Pass to Twin Lakes

To Los Angeles

- - - - - - -
Sierra Crest Tour

- - - - - - -
Trans-Sierra Tour

SIERRA CREST TOURS

Skiing the Sierra Crest is one of the highlights of a ski mountaineer's career. Whether you're tackling the entire reach from Horseshoe Meadows to Twin Lakes or picking one of the shorter stretches along the way, the crest is quite an adventure, like making a low-level flight over some of the most spectacular country on earth. Nowhere else will you find the remarkable blend of weather, terrain, snowpack, and wilderness that characterizes the crest. Add to this the sublime beauty of the Sierra and you have the ultimate backcountry ski experience.

Obviously, you can ski these tours from south to north, or north to south. You should consider the time of year, the snow conditions, and your skill level. Early in the year, it's often best to head north because you climb up transitional south-facing snow and ski down wintry snow on northern aspects. In midspring, it's often best to head south, climbing up the funky north slopes to take advantage of sunny south-facing descents and prime corn snow. By early summer, the south slopes might become patchy and heading north will give you finer downhill runs.

The John Muir Trail forms the basis for skiing the crest, although there are higher and more aesthetic sections. While skiing the entire Sierra Crest is an excellent longterm goal, many folks pick off small sections each year, rather than doing it in one expedition. The Sierra Crest was first skied by Orland Bartholomew (solo, of course) in 1928. It took him just over four months and he preplaced a half-dozen caches along the way.

In 1986, two Outward Bound instructors skied the route in a week on lightweight racing skis. Their first attempt took over a month. To ski the entire route in one push, most folks will require about a month and at least a couple of caches. Because some sections are not as good as others and are extremely snow dependent, you could just focus on the stretch between Muir Pass and Tioga Pass.

The ultimate expression of the Sierra Crest is The Redline, conceived and completed by Allan Bard, Tom Carter, Chris Cox, and Kimberly Walker in 1983. This tour followed the political boundary on the top of the range from Mount Langley to Mammoth Mountain (a red line on their map) and was skied

Ski touring below the Sierra Crest.

using the primitive telemark equipment of the day. The route never strayed more than one-half mile from the actual crest, linking peak after peak and often combining a technical climb with a first ski descent.

The easiest way to access the Crest tours is from the east, but you can combine segments of a Trans-Sierra tour to create a longer trip. You will have to do some form of car shuttle for all of these tours or suffer an epic hitchhike or bike-and-hike to get back to your car. The elevations included in this book are approximate and should give you an idea of the relative gain and loss.

A   Horseshoe Meadows to Onion Valley

Highlights:	Includes the highest section the Sierra Crest and offers a side trip to the summit of Mount Whitney.
Difficulty:	Class 3-4
Distance:	About 45 miles
Trailheads:	Horseshoe Meadows and Onion Valley
USGS 15′ Maps:	Olancha, Mount Whitney
USGS 7.5′ Maps:	Cirque Peak, Johnson Peak, Mount Langley, Mount Whitney, Mount Williamson, Kearsarge Peak

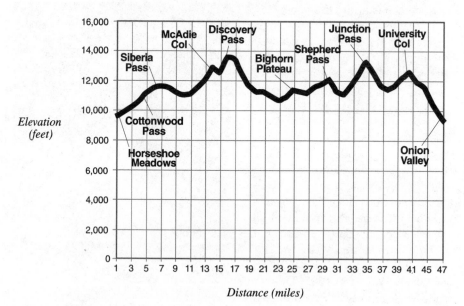

Distance (miles)

Overview: The most southerly section of the Sierra Crest offers the full spectrum of Sierra terrain—flat glacial benches and sheer cliffs, gentle forested

Horseshoe Meadows to Onion Valley

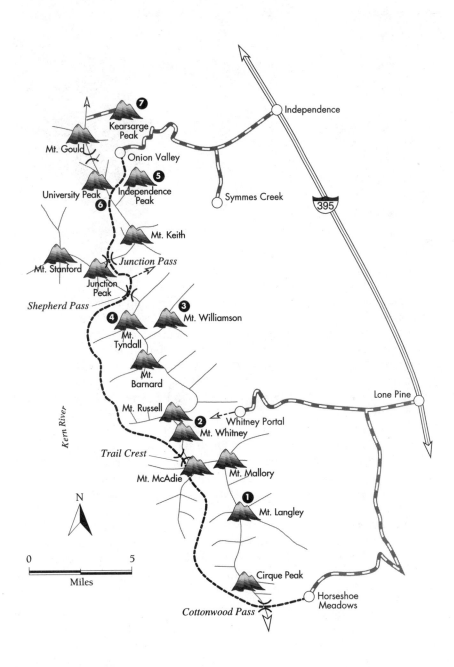

Independence

Kearsarge
Peak

Mt. Gould

Onion Valley

Symmes Creek

University Peak

Independence
Peak

395

Mt. Keith

Junction Pass

Mt. Stanford

Junction
Peak

Shepherd Pass

Mt. Williamson

Mt.
Tyndall

Mt.
Barnard

Kern River

Mt. Russell

Lone Pine

Whitney Portal

Mt. Whitney

Trail Crest

Mt. McAdie

Mt. Mallory

N

Mt. Langley

0   5

Miles

Cirque Peak

Horseshoe
Meadows

Cottonwood Pass

Foxtail pines on Bighorn Plateau. VERN CLEVENGER PHOTO

passes and steep alpine cols. This area rivals The Palisades in height and grandeur, and you get the chance to ski to the summit of Mount Whitney, the highest point in the lower forty-eight. Please note, however, that the rugged barrier of the Kings-Kern Divide provides a challenging obstacle, which can be quite difficult in some years. Rather than attempt the very steep crossing of Forester Pass (13,200'), the highest pass on the John Muir Trail, our route follows the original route of the John Muir Trail over Shepherd Pass and Junction Pass.

Horseshoe Meadows Road is locked early in the season, creating a long walk for anyone who goes too early. Once the road is clear and open, the high trailhead at Horseshoe Meadows allows you to ease into the backcountry with the gentle crossing of Cottonwood Pass before tackling the very high and rugged country around Mount Whitney. North of Mount Whitney, the views are incredible. From Bighorn Plateau, you can see across the deep, glaciated canyon of the Kern River towards the Great Western Divide. Groves of foxtail pines provide excellent shelter for campsites along the way. This long tour can be broken into two segments by using Whitney Portal as an alternate traihead. Also, an optional route tackles a high line over Mount Barnard to the alpine cirque between Mount Tyndall and Mount Williamson.

Route: From the town of Lone Pine on US Highway 395, turn west onto Whitney Portal Road, and then head south on Horseshoe Meadows Road, which ascends the sheer face of the Sierra escarpment via a series of long switchbacks that can be seen from the valley floor. Remember, the gate at the bottom may be locked early in the season, which means a long walk up the road to reach the snow.

30

From the end of the road at Horseshoe Meadows (9,600'), head west and climb gradually through forested, rolling terrain to reach Cottonwood Pass (11,150'). From here, the route begins following the Pacific Crest Trail (PCT), and you will see occasional PCT signs on trees along the way. Follow the PCT as it contours past Chicken Spring Lake through sparse forests to the Rock Creek drainage.

At a trail junction, follow the Siberia Pass Trail (11,100') north up Rock Creek, below Joe Devel Peak and Mount Pickering, to Sky Blue Lake (11,550'). This stunning lake lies between the spectacular tower of The Miter and the jagged eastern ramparts of Mount Pickering. From Sky Blue Lake, follow the unnamed drainage northwest past a high lake and below the south ridge of Mount McAdie to Crabtree Pass (12,550'), which is on the west ridge of Mount McAdie. Drop down a short ways and contour as high as possible below Whitney Pass, then traverse the south slopes of Discovery Pinnacle to reach Trail Crest (13,600').

From here, you can follow the summer trail for 2.5 miles to the summit of Mount Whitney (14,495'). Depending on snow conditions, you may want to cache your skis at Trail Crest and walk to the top. If you are ending your trip here, follow the Whitney Trail down the steep slope on the infamous switchbacks to Trail Camp, continue on past Mirror Lake (10,750'), and finally descend to the trailhead at Whitney Portal (8,400').

To continue from Trail Crest, follow the John Muir Trail down the west slopes of Mount Whitney past Guitar Lake (11,500') and the Crabtree Ranger Station (10,650'), then contour north again past Sandy Meadow (10,650') at the edge of the impressive Kern River Canyon. An easy climb through sparse

Looking north from above Shepherd Pass. CLAUDE FIDDLER PHOTO

trees leads over a saddle (10,960') on the west shoulder of Mount Young ,
then turns east and gradually drops down to cross Wallace Creek (10,400').
The skyline to the west is dominated by the jagged Kaweah Peaks and the
summits of the Great Western Divide.

A short ways to the north, cross Wright Creek (10,650') on the climb up
to Bighorn Plateau (11,200'). Interesting side tours lead east into the basins
that contain Wallace Lakes and Wright Lakes. The route continues along the
west slope of Tawny Point before reaching the timberline at the edge of
barren Tyndall Plateau. Turn east at Tyndall Creek and follow the creek up
a gradual climb to the broad saddle of Shepherd Pass (12,000').

The east side of the pass is quite steep and avalanche-prone, but the angle
soon eases as the route follows the original John Muir Trail down to the
bench (11,200') above The Pothole. The desert of Owens Valley is framed by
the narrow walls of Shepherd Creek Canyon below. The route traverses
below the steep east ridge of Junction Peak, then climbs west up the drainage towards the main summit. Just east of the peak, turn north and climb
the steep slope to reach Junction Pass (13,200').

From Junction Pass, follow the ridge north into Kings Canyon National
Park before dropping down to the lake (12,090') below. A delightful run
down Center Basin eventually brings you to Golden Bear Lake (11,150')
below the pyramid of Center Peak. Cross the basin and make the long steep
climb to University Pass (12,650') on the southeast shoulder of University
Peak. Looking back, the sheer northern wall of the Kings-Kern Divide provides a spectacular backdrop as you prepare for the great descent down the
canyon past Robinson Lake (10,500') and out to the trailhead at Onion Valley (9,200').

B   Onion Valley to South Lake

Highlights:	A high commitment section of the crest visiting a number of beautiful lake basins.
Difficulty:	Class 3-4
Distance:	About 50 miles
Trailheads:	Onion Valley and South Lake
USGS 15' Maps:	Mount Whitney, Mount Pinchot, Big Pine, Mount Goddard
USGS 7.5' Maps:	Kearsarge Peak, Mount Clarence King, Mount Pinchot, Split Mountain, North Palisade, Mount Thompson

Onion Valley to South Lake

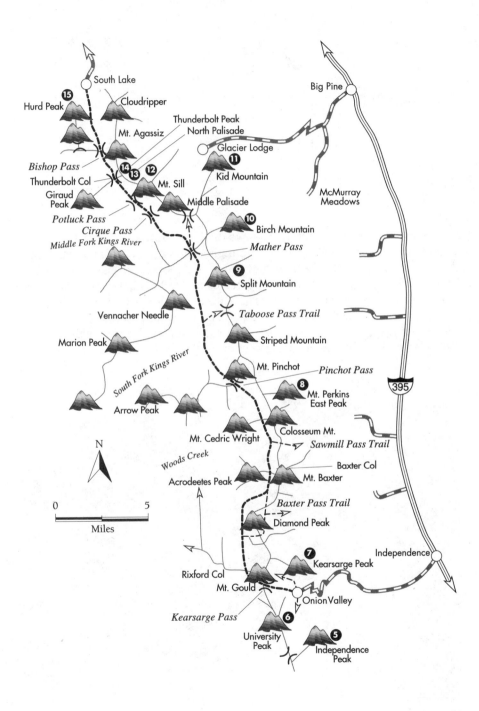

South Lake

⑮ Hurd Peak

Cloudripper

Thunderbolt Peak
North Palisade

Mt. Agassiz

Big Pine

Glacier Lodge ⑪

Bishop Pass

⑭ ⑬ ⑫

Kid Mountain

Thunderbolt Col

Mt. Sill

*Giraud
Peak*

Middle Palisade

McMurray
Meadows

Potluck Pass
Cirque Pass
Middle Fork Kings River

⑩ Birch Mountain

Mather Pass

⑨ Split Mountain

Vennacher Needle

Taboose Pass Trail

Marion Peak

Striped Mountain

South Fork Kings River

Mt. Pinchot *Pinchot Pass*

395

⑧ Mt. Perkins
East Peak

Arrow Peak

Colosseum Mt.

Mt. Cedric Wright

Sawmill Pass Trail

N

Woods Creek

Baxter Col

Acrodeetes Peak

Mt. Baxter

Baxter Pass Trail

0   5
Miles

Diamond Peak

Independence

⑦ Kearsarge Peak

Rixford Col

Mt. Gould

Onion Valley

Kearsarge Pass

⑥

⑤

University
Peak

Independence
Peak

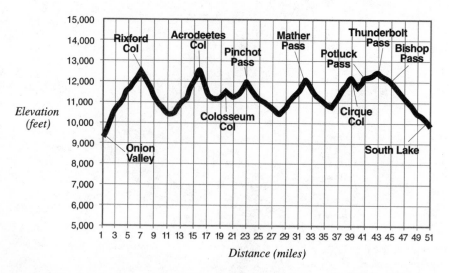

Elevation (feet)

Rixford Col

Acrodeetes Col

Pinchot Pass

Mather Pass

Thunderbolt Pass

Potluck Pass

Bishop Pass

Colosseum Col

Cirque Col

Onion Valley

South Lake

Distance (miles)

Overview: This route generally follows the John Muir Trail with the exception of two detours that keep the line higher along the crest and avoid the disappointing drops to the low elevations of Woods and Palisade creeks. This high line hugs the crest from Baxter Lakes to Twin Lakes and traverses along the western escarpment of The Palisades. Along the way, this spectacular route travels through Rae Lakes, The Palisades, and Dusy Basin before heading out over Bishop Pass. The route across the west side of The Palisades may be the most scenic section of the entire crest. A trip on this

Looking south from the head of Kings River. VERN CLEVENGER PHOTO.

Skiing off the north side of Mather Pass.

section of the crest is greatly influenced by seasonal conditions because the first part can be thin in low snow years.

Route: The route leaves Onion Valley (9,200') and follows the John Muir Trail up to Kearsarge Pass (11,800'). From the pass, the route traverses northwest into Kings Canyon National Park over the west shoulder of Mount Gould (13,005') and toward Mount Rixford. A steep drop from the obvious col (12,450') brings you to the trio of lakes (11,800') west of Dragon Peak before dropping you farther down to Dragon Lake (11,100'). For an alternate route, ski up to Golden Trout Lake from Onion Valley, over the steep Gould Pass (12,800') just north of the summit of Mount Gould, and then down to the three lakes.

From Dragon Lake, the route drops into the gorgeous basin of Rae Lakes (10,550'). Continue the gentle descent until near Dollar Lake (10,250'), then take the Baxter Pass Trail around the west slope of Diamond Peak and up to the largest of the Baxter Lakes (11,150'). Enjoy great views back to the west toward Mount Clarence King and Mount Cotter on your ascent.

At the Baxter Lakes, the route lines up for the gunsights—two similar passes that lie directly in line with each other. The first climb heads up the steep slope to Baxter Col (12,500') between Mount Baxter and Acrodectes Peak. After a steep drop to Stocking Lake (11,400'), follow the headwaters of Woods Creek down to Woods Lake (10,750'), where an alternate trail heads over Sawmill Pass to Owens Valley.

From Woods Lake, the route heads north and climbs up to the col just east of Mount Cedric Wright (11,600'). After a short drop, follow the drainage down to Twin Lakes (10,600'). The route heads north below Mount Perkins, joins the John Muir Trail just south of Mount Wynne, and climbs

Touring below the west side of The Palisades.

up to Pinchot Pass (12,100'). A great descent from the pass brings you past Lake Marjory (11,150') and down to the crossing of the South Fork of Kings River (10,200'). Westward, the great pyramid of Arrow Peak sits across South Fork Kings River Canyon from the remote Monarch Divide. To the east, the broad saddle of Taboose Pass (11,400') offers an escape route down to Owens Valley.

A lengthy but gentle climb takes you along the South Fork of Kings River into the huge Upper Basin (11,200'). On the east margin of the basin, the north slopes of Split Mountain (14,058') offer a fine, long ski descent. At the north end of the basin, begin the steep climb to Mather Pass (12,100'), which often involves surmounting a sizeable cornice at the top. The north side of the pass begins steeply but soon becomes more gentle and provides a great run down to the bench above Palisade Lakes (11,200'). From here, you can exit over the very steep Southfork Pass (12,600') and out to Glacier Lodge (7,800').

Our route, however, continues down to the western end of the lowest of the Palisade Lakes (10,600'), then turns north for the spectacular tour along the western escarpment of The Palisades. From the lake, an easy climb up moderate slopes leads northwest to the obvious saddle of Cirque Pass (12,100') and the steep run down to the lake (11,675') at the head of Glacier Creek. The side trip up Mount Sill (14,162') is highly recommended. Steep ledges climb from the lake over Potluck Pass (12,150') and onto the broad bench that traverses below the sheer west face of North Palisade. The view west over the Palisade Basin towards the remote backcountry of Kings Canyon is truly breathtaking, as ridge after ridge of isolated peaks stretch out to the horizon.

Continuing north, a short climb takes you to Thunderbolt Col (12,400') at the foot of the rugged southwest ridge of Thunderbolt Peak. From the pass, an easy traverse north leads to Bishop Pass (11,950'). Most folks opt for a detour into Dusy Basin and camp at the very scenic lake (11,400') at the foot of Isosceles Peak. From the lake, a moderate climb takes you back up to the low saddle of Bishop Pass, where there are great views towards the sheer west faces of The Palisades. Black Divide and the ominous Devils Crags loom across deep LeConte Canyon. A short but steep descent brings you to Bishop Lake (11,250) at the foot of the great ski slopes of Mount Goode (13,085'). From here, a gentle run down the South Fork of Bishop Creek takes you past Long Lake (10,750') and out to the trailhead at South Lake (9,750').

C South Lake to North Lake

Highlights: A challenging tour requiring good routefinding skills to negotiate this spectacularly technical terrain.
Difficulty: Class 4
Distance: About 35 miles
Trailheads: South Lake and North Lake
USGS 15' Maps: Mount Goddard
USGS 7.5' Maps: Mount Thompson, Mount Darwin, Mount Goddard

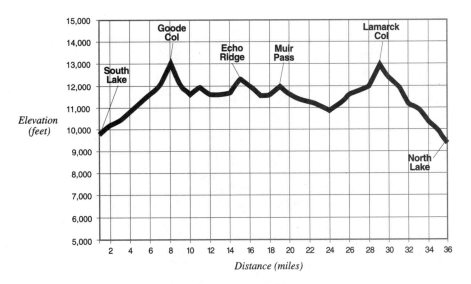

Overview: The loop from South Lake to North Lake is considered a classic Sierra summer backpacking trip. In the winter, it is much more difficult, especially if you try to stay high on the crest rather than following the John

South Lake to North Lake

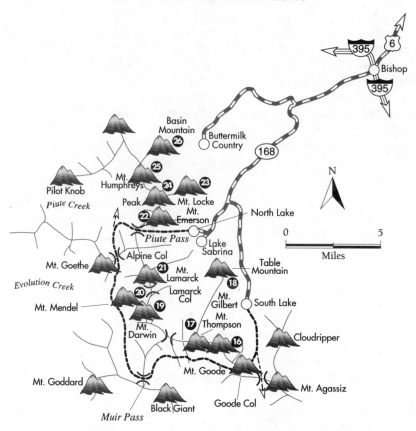

Muir Trail down into LeConte Canyon. This trip begins with a wonderful traverse of South Lake and Lake Sabrina basins before crossing Muir Pass at the heart of the High Sierra. The highlight of this tour is the gentle run down through beautiful Evolution Basin and up into rugged Darwin Canyon. This is one of the most difficult sections of the crest, but it is also one of the most dramatic and rewarding. Are ready for the challenge?

Route: The tour begins at the high trailhead of South Lake (9,750') and follows the South Fork of Bishop Creek up benches to the south end of Long Lake (10,750'). Directly to the south, the sheer face of Mount Goode dominates the view. Rather than heading over Bishop Pass, continue climbing along the creek to Saddlerock Lake (11,125'), then head up into the cirque on the south side of Mount Goode. You reach the col (12,700') just south of the summit (13,085'). The run back down the bowl to Saddlerock Lake is an excellent ski descent and worth the extra trip.

From the col, the route drops west down a very steep couloir (The Elevator Shaft) into the large cirque west of Mount Goode and ends at the small lake (11,350') just south of Mount Johnson. Follow the outlet creek down a short way before heading up the open slope to the west and across the low shoulder of the south ridge of Mount Johnson (11,900'). A very steep cliff guards the route west down to the creek (11,000') that drains the south side of Mount Gilbert, and sometimes a cornice blocks the way. You can also reach this point from South Lake via the Treasures Lakes (10,650') and the very steep col (12,400') on the ridge between Mount Gilbert and Mount Johnson.

The route follows the obvious bench system on the south side of the crest and eventually ascends to the large lake (11,725') on the south side of Mount Powell. Along this section, the short ridges that drop south from the crest keep things interesting, and these spurs can provide some exciting routefinding. The reward for your effort is the view south down spectacular LeConte Canyon, which is one of the finest in the range. From the lake south of Mount Powell, ski up the cirque towards the west summit of Mount Powell before climbing onto the steep south ridge (12,300'). A steep gully drops you onto the large lake (11,425') at the base of Echo Col.

From the lake, the route drops down to the John Muir Trail (11,000') before climbing past Helen Lake (11,600') to the stone shelter at Muir Pass (11,950'). There really is no reason to keep a high line at this point. The Muir Hut makes a good base (although a tad chilly) for skiing Mount Theodore Solomons (13,034') or Black Giant (13,330') to the south or for exploring Evolution and Ionian basins. The dark cone of Mount Goddard presides over the gentle slopes leading past Wanda Lake (11,400') and Sapphire Lake (11,000') to Evolution Lake (10,850'), one of the most beautiful locations in the entire range.

Skiing across Helen Lake. JIM STIMSON PHOTO

Touring in Evolution Basin below Muir Pass. JIM STIMSON PHOTO

From the north end of the lake, contour around the west ridge of Mount Mendel and climb into spectacular Darwin Canyon (11,200'). Looking west, The Hermit stands guard over broad Evolution Basin and the obviously glaciated Evolution Valley. There is no straightforward route over Glacier Divide at this point, so our route heads up Darwin Canyon to the highest of the lakes (11,900') below Lamarck Col (12,900'). This pass provides an alternate route out and leads to North Lake (9,400'). From a base at the head of Darwin Canyon, the north face of Mount Darwin provides a very compelling and challenging ski descent, while the twin ice gullies on the north face of Mount Mendel provide classic ice climbs, as well as ultimate extreme descents for the truly twisted.

Our route heads north to the lakes south of Muriel Peak. A steep climb leads up to either Alpine Col (12,350') on the west side of Muriel Peak or The Keyhole (12,550') to the east of Muriel Peak. These passes are about equal in difficulty, so pick your poison. In either case, a moderate descent drops north down through the scenic Goethe Cirque to Muriel Lake (11,350').

From Muriel Lake, the huge mass of Mount Humphreys dominates the northern skyline. Piute Pass (11,425') is the low saddle to the east, which is reached by a simple contour. Drop down the east side of the pass into the broad valley below, passing Piute Lake (10,950') and Loch Leven (10,750'). Then drop steeply down into the aspens of the lower canyon below colorful Piute Crags and out to North Lake (9,400'). An alternate route out of Darwin Canyon leads up over Lamarck Col (13,000'), drops down to the Lamarck Lakes, and eventually reaches North Lake.

D North Lake to Rock Creek

Highlights:	Prime touring terrain and an excellent introduction to long backcountry tours.
Difficulty:	Class 3
Distance:	About 35 miles
Trailheads:	North Lake and Rock Creek
USGS 15′ Maps:	Mount Tom, Mount Abbot, Mount Morgan
USGS 7.5′ Maps:	Mount Darwin, Mount Tom, Mount Hilgard, Mount Abbot, Mount Morgan

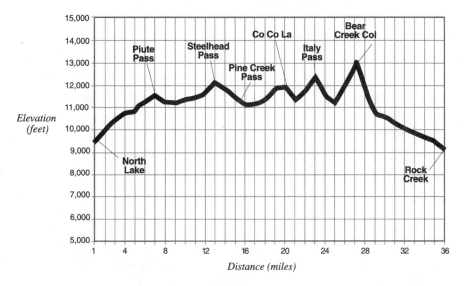

Overview: This popular section of crest is an excellent tour in its own right. The character of the crest changes at Piute Pass, where the open expanses of

Mount Humphreys above Humphreys Basin.

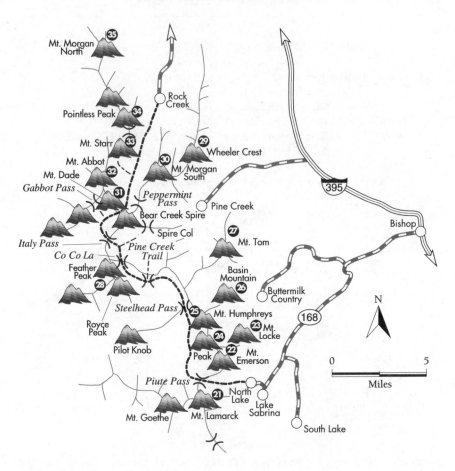

Humphreys Basin replace the jagged peaks of the Evolution group, and the crest is now dominated by the towering mass of Mount Humphreys. The tour regains its alpine character as it passes beneath the huge rock faces of the Royce peaks and the spectacular spires surrounding Granite Park and Rock Creek Canyon, but much of the terrain is still open and gentle.

This is classic touring terrain and there are many options for layovers to explore Humphreys Basin and Granite Park and to climb the fine peaks around Royce Lakes and Lake Italy. This tour is perhaps the easiest section of the crest; moderate passes provide a very skiable route throughout the entire length. At one time, the guides from Alpine Expeditions and Rock Creek Winter Lodge, led by Allan Bard, had a series of fully stocked camps along this section of the crest, which allowed their guests to ski the route with day packs—true alpine touring.

Route: The route begins at North Lake (9,400') and follows the summer trail that ascends through a forest of aspens below colorful Piute Crags.

Eventually, a short, steep traverse through a prominent cliff band brings you to Loch Leven (10,750'). The route follows the broad valley past Piute Lake (10,950') before making the final short climb to Piute Pass (11,425').

From the pass, contour north past Summit Lake (11,200') and into the drainage leading to Lower Desolation Lake (11,200'). To the south, the sheer escarpment of Glacier Divide provides a dramatic backdrop. A short climb north brings you to expansive Desolation Lake (11,375') at the foot of Mount Humphreys.

From the lake, angle northeast towards the saddle where the prominent divide meets the crest at Steelhead Pass (11,560'). The other passes on the divide are steeper and may involve negotiating cornices. From the pass, a steep slope drops north toward Steelhead Lake (10,400'). A gentle sidehill traverse leads west past the outlet creek of French Lake (11,200') and on to the broad saddle of Pine Creek Pass (11,150'). In the distance to the north, the white granite of Bear Creek Spire contrasts sharply with the zebra-striped cliffs above Pine Creek. From the pass, it is possible to end the tour via the fun descent down to Upper Pine Lake (9,950'). However, during periods of high avalanche hazard, the trip down Pine Creek Canyon to Pine Creek Road (7,500') can become much too dangerous to attempt.

The next section of the crest is not to be missed. Ascend the moderate slope to the west of Pine Creek Pass to reach stunning Royce Lakes (11,700'). There are excellent bowls to ski here, as well as fun descents of Merriam Peak (13,077'), Royce Peak (13,253'), and Feather Peak (13,242'). Leaving Royce Lakes, the low saddle (the Co Co La) between the impressive rock buttresses of Spire Peak and Bear Claw Spire takes you down into the lower reaches of the exceptionally beautiful Granite Park. Although it is possible to continue north and cross the east ridge of Bear Creek Spire to reach Rock Creek Canyon, this route involves some technical climbing (class 4-5). Instead, our route heads west through the upper bowls of Granite Park to reach Italy Pass. The gentle climb through this huge basin passes a number of unnamed granite spires before reaching Italy Pass (12,400') at the foot of Mount Julius Caesar (13,200').

Looking south over Royce Lakes and Granite Park.

Looking south over Pine Creek Pass to Glacier Divide from Chalfant Lakes.

From the pass, the route descends west to Jumble Lake (11,500') and down into the stark basin of Lake Italy (11,200'), which is rimmed by the great hulks of Mount Hilgard, Mount Gabb, Mount Abbot, and Mount Dade. Traversing around to Toe Lake, the route slogs up the broad slopes to the north before heading east to the high crest crossing (13,050') just north of Bear Creak Spire. Don't head for the low point of the saddle, but rather to a point a few hundred feet to the north, because this leads to an easier descent on the east side. A highly recommended side trip from the pass follows the obvious talus slopes to the final short cliff guarding the summit of Bear Creek Spire (13,713').

From the pass, the route descends an unnamed glacier into Rock Creek Canyon, passing below the north arête of Bear Creek Spire, as well as Dade Lake (11,600'), on the way to the timberline bowls surrounding the Treasure Lakes (11,175'). A gentle descent from the outlet of the lakes takes you down scenic Little Lakes Valley past Long Lake (10,550') and Mack Lake (10,350') to Mosquito Flats (10,200'). A final run down the Rock Creek Road takes you past Rock Creek Lake (9,700') and the Rock Creek Lodge to the beginning of Rock Creek Road at East Fork Campground (8,900').

E Rock Creek to Mammoth

Highlights: A scenic tour offering great skiing and a number of opportunities for layover camps.
Difficulty: Class 3-4
Distance: About 35 miles
Trailheads: Rock Creek and Tamarack Lodge
USGS 15′ Maps: Mount Abbot, Mount Morrison
USGS 7.5′ Maps: Mount Morgan, Mount Abbot, Convict Lake, Bloody Mountain, Crystal Crag

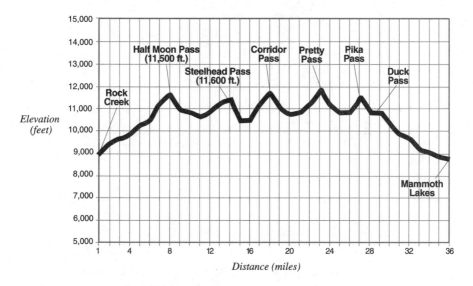

Overview: This trip offers some of the best backcountry skiing in the High Sierra. The scenery ranges from the spectacular granite spires of Rock Creek Canyon to the sublime beauty of Pioneer Basin. The colors of the Convict Lake area are unforgettable. There are many opportunities for shorter tours in this region and alternative routes abound. Also, many interesting ski descents, including Red Slate Mountain, are easily accessible from this route.

Although this route is one of the tougher sections of the crest, it has been skied many times in a day. There are six major passes on the

Touring below Red Slate Mountain.

45

Rock Creek to Mammoth

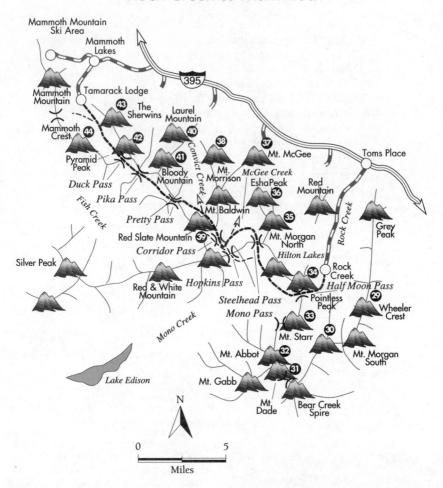

route and some of these involve steep climbing and icy conditions. During periods of high avalanche hazard, this tour is very dangerous. On the positive side, Corridor Pass, which links McGee and Convict canyons, is one of the most amazing ski passes you'll ever find. All in all, this fine tour is one of the best ski mountaineering trips anywhere.

Route: This tour starts from the beginning of Rock Creek Road (8,900') and follows the road past Rock Creek Lake (9,700') to Mosquito Flats (10,200'). From here, follow Ruby Creek to Ruby Lake (11,125'), then contour around the south buttress of Mount Starr to Mono Pass (12,050'). The views from the pass back to Mount Abbot and Bear Creek Spire are terrific, but the views to the north are disappointing until you begin dropping down to Golden Lake (11,000'). There is a shortcut from Rock Creek Lake west over Half Moon Pass (11,480') and directly down to Golden Lake, but this route is

Touring in Hopkins Basin.

more difficult and involves very steep snow, some rock scrambling, and potentially high avalanche hazard.

From Golden Lake, contour along the north side of Mono Creek until you can traverse to the lake at the mouth of Pioneer Basin (10,400'). Ascend the drainage to the largest of the lakes in the middle of the basin (10,800'). There are excellent views back across Mono Creek to Mount Mills and the great hanging valleys of the Mono Recesses. From the lakes, continue north up the drainage to the obvious saddle of Steelhead Pass (11,560'). The north side of the pass is very steep and often blocked by a cornice. Usually, you can find a reasonable route by checking to one side or the other.

The bowl eventually opens up below the pass as it reaches Steelhead Lake (10,400'). Skirt the west side of the lake and contour around below the north slopes of Mount Crocker to reach Big McGee Lake (10,500'). It is also possible to reach the lake by touring into Hopkins Basin, but the route over Hopkins Pass is very steep and often involves trying to find a reasonable way around the summit cornices.

From Big McGee Lake, the route climbs steadily into the hourglass-shaped valley to the north and soon reaches well-named Corridor Pass (11,800') about a mile east of Red Slate Mountain. From the pass, there are great views back across McGee Creek Canyon; look to the north to see colorful Convict Creek Canyon. A wonderful descent takes you through open bowls down to Constance Lake (10,800'), which lies below the great north face of Red Slate Mountain. From here, you can shorten the tour by skiing out Convict Creek Canyon to Convict Lake (7,600').

Red Slate Mountain above Corridor Pass.

Looking east from the summit of Red Slate Mountain.

The route continues, traversing the head of Convict Canyon. Looking across teardrop-shaped Dorothy Lake, the colorful slopes of Mount Baldwin and Mount Morrison reveal the extreme geological forces that shaped this area. A final difficult climb leads west up steeper slopes to the narrow col of Pretty Pass (11,900'). From the pass, a steep drop leads down to the Franklin Lakes (11,150'), then a gentle run takes you across to Ram Lake (10,800').

From the lake, climb steeply toward the narrow notch where a prominent ridge joins the main crest at Pika Pass (11,575'). This climb is often icy, and crampons will probably make you feel more secure. From the pass, drop down a short way until you can contour above the east shores of Duck Lake (10,475') to Duck Pass (10,800'). A short but steep descent on the north side leads into the open bowls surrounding Barney Lake (10,200'), which lies at the head of Mammoth Creek. Follow the creek down past Skelton Lake (9,900') and Arrowhead Lake (9,675') to a final steep, forested slope above Coldwater Campground (9,000). Finally, groomed trails lead to the trailhead at Tamarack Lodge (8,700').

F   Mammoth to Tioga Pass

Highlights: A popular tour with relatively easy touring terrain.
Difficulty: Class 3
Distance: About 40 miles
Trailheads: Tamarack Lodge and Tioga Pass Resort
USGS 15′ Maps: Devils Postpile, Mono Craters, Tuolumne Meadows
USGS 7.5′ Maps: Mammoth Mountain, Mount Ritter, Koip Peak, Tioga Pass, Mount Dana

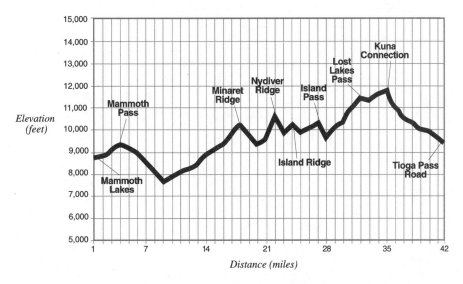

Overview: This route is not truly a Sierra Crest tour because it leaves the main crest to traverse the more spectacular Ritter Range to the west. The Sierra Crest in this area stays pretty low and lacks the alpine character of

The Minarets and Ritter Range.

Mammoth to Tioga Pass

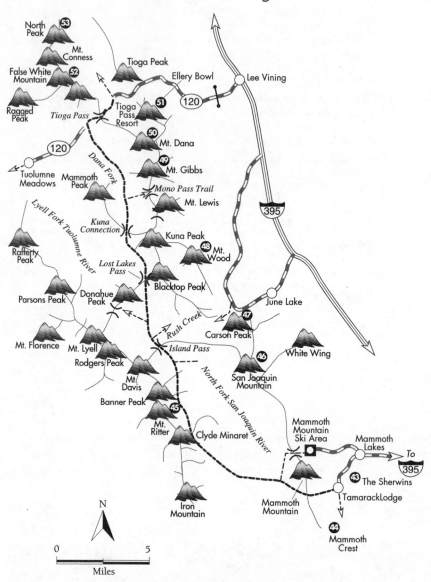

the rest of the Crest tours; however, the Ritter Range has everything: The scenery is fantastic and the route finds skiable passes right along the base of the spectacular Minarets. Although you must drop low while crossing the San Joaquin River to reach The Minarets, a hot spring along the way usually appeases even the most hardcore altitude junkie. The route also takes a higher and more enjoyable line into Yosemite National Park, catching California 120 at Dana Meadows, which makes it an excellent alternative to the popular Mammoth to Yosemite trans-Sierra tour.

Touring across Thousand Island Lake. VERN CLEVENGER PHOTO

Route: From Tamarack Lodge (8,700'), follow the groomed trail to Horseshoe Lake (9,000') before climbing through trees to the low saddle of Mammoth Pass (9,300'). A fine descent drops down through the burned forest and leads to the hot spring at Reds Meadow (7,600'). Continue north on the summer trail to the unusual geologic formation of Devils Postpile. Cross the San Joaquin River at the bridge or at the broad ford just north of the Postpile, then follow the summer trail up through forested benchlands to the junction with the John Muir Trail at Johnson Meadow (8,000'). Continue west on the north side of Minaret Creek to reach the shores of spectacular Minaret Lake (9,800'). Clyde Minaret towers over the route as you climb a short headwall onto the bench above, which holds Cecile Lake (10,250'). A short steep descent brings you to Iceberg Lake (9,775') and then on to the very beautiful Ediza Lake (9,350').

From Ediza Lake, a steep climb leads north up to Nydiver Lakes (10,100'), which lie at the base of the great bowl between Mount Ritter and Banner Peak. Cross the east ridge of Banner Peak at the low saddle to the north (10,500'), then traverse down to the small lake just west of Garnet Lake (9,800'). A short climb takes you over another low saddle (10,150') and down onto huge Thousand Island Lake (9,800'). Another short climb through the trees to the north quickly brings you to Island Pass (10,150').

A gentle descent leads northwest from the pass down to the forested forks of Rush Creek (9,650'). Cross the creek well above Waugh Lake. From Rush Creek, follow the John Muir Trail northwest until you near a prominent knob about a mile east of Donahue Pass, then follow the next drainage

Looking south up the Dana Fork to Kuna Crest.

north to the largest of the Lost Lakes (10,950'). From the lake, a moderate climb leads up to Lost Lakes Pass (11,400') below the dark spires of Black-top Peak and Koip Crest.

Now you are in Yosemite National Park. Traverse northwest across the huge plateau above Kuna Creek until you are on the west side of the Kuna Crest, passing below the prominent southwest spur of Kuna Peak. Kuna Pass (11,800') is the broad saddle just south of Helen Lake. The top of the pass is often blocked by a cornice, but the angle of the bowl below quickly eases and brings you down to Helen Lake (10,950').

From the lake, the route continues down Parker Creek past Spillway Lake (10,450') to Dana Meadows (9,600'). From the meadows, follow CA 120 over Tioga Pass (9,945') and down to Tioga Pass Resort (9,550'). In late spring, Lee Vining Canyon Road may be plowed to this point. Normally, you'll have an 8-mile descent to Lee Vining Campground (7,400'). This road can have extreme avalanche and rockfall hazard, so don't linger on the road, especially late in the day.

G   Tioga Pass to Twin Lakes

Highlights:	A short tour with the chance to ski over the summits of two major peaks.
Difficulty:	Class 3
Distance:	About 25 miles
Trailheads:	Tioga Pass Resort and Twin Lakes
USGS 15′ Maps:	Tuolumne Meadows, Matterhorn Peak
USGS 7.5′ Maps:	Tioga Pass, Dunderberg Peak

Tioga Pass to Twin Lakes

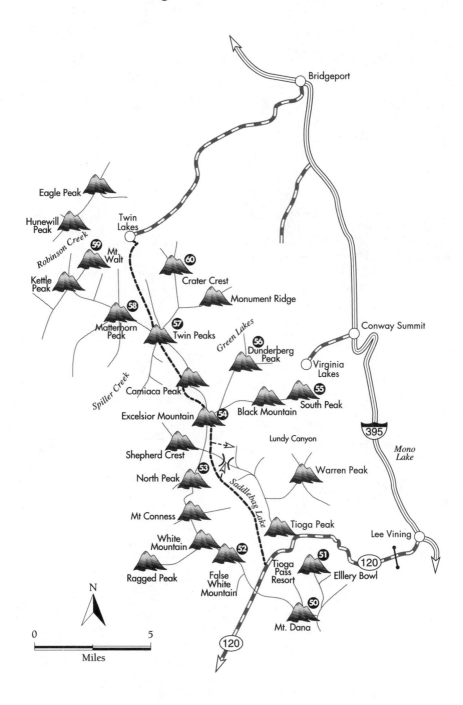

Bridgeport

Eagle Peak

Hunewill Peak

Twin Lakes

Robinson Creek

59 Mt. Walt

60

Crater Crest

Monument Ridge

Conway Summit

Kettle Peak

58

Matterhorn Peak

57 Twin Peaks

Green Lakes

56 Dunderberg Peak

Virginia Lakes

Spiller Creek

Camiaca Peak

55 South Peak

54 Black Mountain

Excelsior Mountain

Lundy Canyon

395

Mono Lake

Shepherd Crest

53

North Peak

Saddlebag Lake

Warren Peak

Mt Conness

White Mountain

Tioga Peak

Lee Vining

52

120

Ragged Peak

False White Mountain

51 Tioga Pass Resort

Elllery Bowl

50 Mt. Dana

N

0   5
Miles

120

Camp in Twenty Lakes Basin below North Peak.

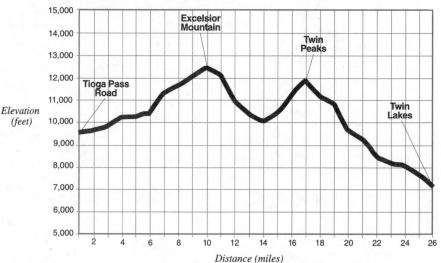

Overview: Although this route is shorter than the other tours in this section, it's a backcountry skier's dream—the solitude of the seldom-visited northern part of Yosemite National Park and the many bowl-skiing opportunities along the way. The route climbs two 12,000-foot peaks that have excellent views and tremendous ski descents from their summits. Finally, the ski run down Horse Creek Canyon is one of the finest in the range.

You could easily do this tour in two days, but you really should allow more time to enjoy areas like Twenty Lakes Basin, Summit Lake, and Virginia Pass. Also, you could tie this tour in with a high traverse of Sawtooth Ridge and come out at Robinson Creek. Finally, there are good reasons for doing this route in the other direction. Heading south, the downhill run from Excelsior Peak to Saddlebag Lake is almost as good as the run down Horse Creek Canyon.

Route: It's best to wait until the Tioga Pass Road is plowed to the Tioga Pass Resort (9,550') before beginning this tour. From Tioga Pass Resort, follow the road up to Saddlebag Lake (10,200') past the open bowls of White Mountain and Mount Conness. Skirt around the west shore of the lake toward jagged North Peak, then on to Steelhead Lake (10,400') in the alpine setting of Twenty Lakes Basin. Although camping is prohibited in the Hall Natural Area to the southwest, it is allowed here.

Saddlebag Ridge.

The route then skirts the cliffs at the head of Lundy Canyon before

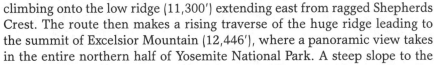

climbing onto the low ridge (11,300') extending east from ragged Shepherds Crest. The route then makes a rising traverse of the huge ridge leading to the summit of Excelsior Mountain (12,446'), where a panoramic view takes in the entire northern half of Yosemite National Park. A steep slope to the northeast provides an excellent descent off the north peak of Excelsior and down to either Onion Lake (10,400') or the head of Green Creek (10,300'). A short traverse around either side of a prominent pyramid brings you to stunning Summit Lake (10,200'). From here, the route traverses around the west slopes of Camiaca Peak to the head of classic, U-shaped Virginia Canyon (10,200'), just below the spectacular towers of Virginia Peak.

The large black mass of Twin Peaks blocks the view to the north. Follow the drainage to the east of the peak to just below the eastern summit of the peak (11,900'). A very steep descent drops down the easternmost of the two steep couloirs on the east side of the peak to the glacier (11,300') below. A short

Looking back at Excelsior Peak from Twin Peaks.

55

Twin Peaks from Excelsior Peak.

traverse over a low ridge takes you from the drainage of Cattle Creek onto the glacier at the head of Horse Creek Canyon. This huge natural half-pipe provides an excellent descent to the flat meadows of Horse Creek (8,300') far below. From the meadows, follow the summer trail and switchback down past Horse Creek Falls to the end of the road at Twin Lakes (7,100').

Trans-Sierra Tours

Trans-Sierra Tours

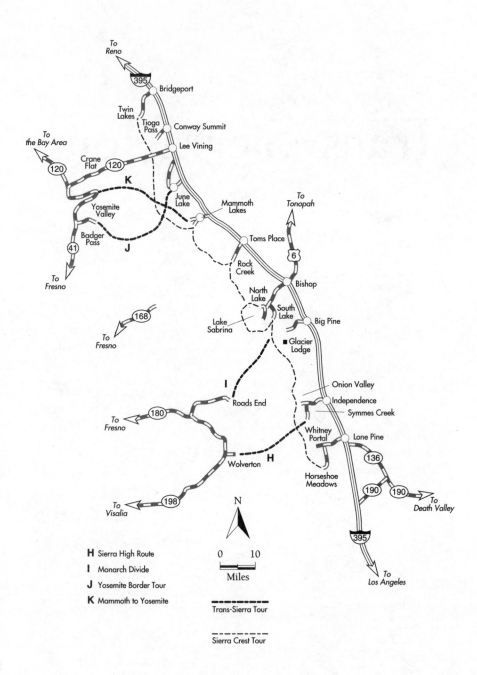

To Reno

395 Bridgeport

Twin Lakes

Tioga Pass

Conway Summit

Lee Vining

To the Bay Area

Crane Flat

120 120

K

June Lake

Mammoth Lakes

To Tonopah

Yosemite Valley

Badger Pass

41

J

Toms Place

6

To Fresno

Rock Creek

North Lake

South Lake

Bishop

168

Lake Sabrina

To Fresno

■ Glacier Lodge

Big Pine

Onion Valley

Independence

I

Roads End

Symmes Creek

180

To Fresno

Whitney Portal

Lone Pine

136

H

Wolverton

Horseshoe Meadows

190

190

To Death Valley

198

To Visalia

N

0   10
Miles

395

To Los Angeles

H Sierra High Route

I Monarch Divide

J Yosemite Border Tour

K Mammoth to Yosemite

- - - - - Trans-Sierra Tour

– – – – – Sierra Crest Tour

TRANS-SIERRA TOURS

For many folks, skiing across the Sierra is even more fun than taking to the crest of the range. Trans-Sierra tours tackle the great divides that separate major river drainages such as the Kern, Kaweah, Kings, San Joaquin, and Merced. In almost every case, these tours are generally more committing than a Sierra Crest tour because each has a point of no return. Once you reach the halfway point on a trans-Sierra tour, it's usually easier to continue on than to turn back. In addition, you're about as far from civilization as you can get these days in the lower forty-eight. Self-reliance is of the utmost importance on these trips.

Aside from the terrain, the main challenge of a trans-Sierra tour is logistics. How do you get back across the range if you've left your car at the trailhead? Various solutions work with varying degrees of success and efficiency. First, you can do a massive driving tour of California by taking two cars to the tour's finish and leaving one. You'll have a car waiting for you at the end of your trip, but you'll have to repeat the process to retrieve the car at the start. An interesting option is to split your party in two and have half the group ski one way and half ski the other. The trick is to meet in the middle somewhere and exchange car keys.

The simplest way to get back is to ski back. Either retrace the route or ski back across on another trans-Sierra tour. The easiest return tours are Bubbs Creek (from Cedar Grove to Onion Valley), Mono Creek (from Huntington Lake to Rock Creek), and Tioga Pass Road (from Crane Flat to Lee Vining). Each of these loops provides a reasonable trip for a long weekend. As a last resort, you could ski across and then try hitchhiking, buses, walking, or even charter a plane to get back. I don't recommend this. I've had some ridiculous epics that were never worth the effort.

As with the Crest tours, I've chosen to present only the most popular and representative trans-Sierra tours. There are others that I'll leave to your imagination. I've also picked a direction for these tours based solely on my own prejudice. Going east to west at least gives the impression that you are starting high and ending low for a mostly downhill tour, but this never seems to work out in real life. Also, as with the sections in this book, the elevations included are approximate and should give you an idea of the relative gain and loss.

Topping out in Cloud Canyon, Sierra High Route.

H   Sierra High Route

Highlights: Justifiably the most famous ski tour in the range.
Difficulty: Class 3-4
Distance: About 45 miles
Trailheads: Symmes Creek and Wolverton Ski Area
USGS 15' Maps: Mount Whitney, Triple Divide Peak
USGS 7.5' Maps: Mount Williamson, Mount Brewer, Mount Kaweah, Triple Divide Peak, Lodgepole

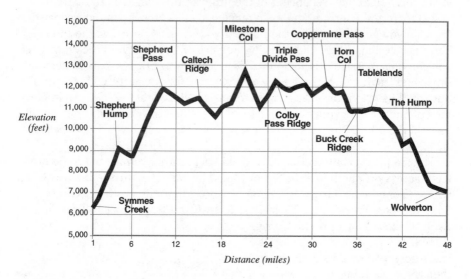

Distance (miles)

Overview: This classic trans-Sierra tour is goal of most Sierra backcountry skiers. The Sierra High Route has everything—wonderful high traverses, great ski descents, spectacular scenery, and exciting mountaineering chal-lenges. This tour, which justifiably ranks as one of the finest ski tours in the world, enjoys a rich history. A variation of this route was done in the early 1930s, but the classic route was first done by pioneering guides David and Susan Beck in the mid-1970s. Over the past 20 years, the High Route has become very popular.

The route basically follows the boundary between Sequoia and Kings Canyon national parks along the divide between the Kings, Kern, and Kaweah rivers. Starting in the high desert, the route quickly rises to over 12,000 feet and stays above 11,000 feet for most of the tour before dropping into the giant sequoias on the west side. There are tremendous views all along the route, but especially in Cloud and Deadman canyons.

Route: The route begins in the high desert at the the trailhead at Symmes Creek (6,300'). You more of less follow the summer trail up steep switchbacks over a saddle (9,400') and into the drainage of Shepherd Creek. The trail traverses down across a steep, sandy slope before reaching the creek at

Sierra High Route

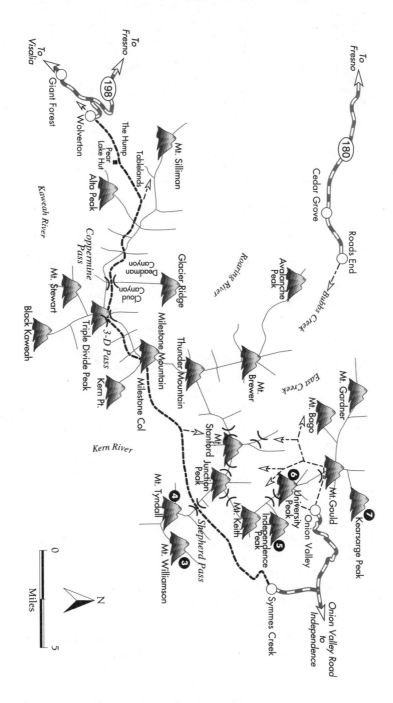

Traversing the head of Kern-Kaweah Canyon.

Mahogany Flat (9,000'). From here, the route follows the creek up past Anvil Camp (10,000') and The Pothole (10,800') before reaching the moraine below Shepherd Pass. The final slope up to the pass (12,000') is quite steep and can be avalanche-prone. Beware.

At the pass, you enter Sequoia National Park. A gentle descent from the pass brings you out onto the open, sparsely timbered slopes of Tyndall Plateau (11,700'). Contour around the toe of Diamond Mesa, then head west toward the low saddle (11,500') at the end of the ridge trending south from Lake South America. From here, drop down steep, forested benches to the small lakes near the head of Kern River Canyon (10,650').

For an alternate start to the tour, begin at Onion Valley (9,200'). This route leads over Kearsarge Pass (11,800') and down past Bullfrog Lake (10,600') to Bubbs Creek Trail at Vidette Meadows (8,300'). From here, you can ski up Vidette Creek Canyon past the Vidette Lakes (10,500') to Deerhorn Saddle (12,600'), where you can look across the Ericsson Lakes (11,800') cirque to the steep climbs leading over Harrison Pass (12,800') or Ericsson Pass (12,600') to the Kern River and the High Route. This start begins at a higher trailhead and adds some very wild terrain.

From the Kern, follow the course of Milestone Creek up into beautiful Milestone Basin (11,200'). To the east, the 14,000-foot summits of Mount Langley, Mount Muir, Mount Whitney, Mount Russell, Mount Tyndall, and Mount Williamson line the crest and preside over the canyon of the Kern. To the west, at the head of the basin, locate the sharp granite spire of Milestone Peak. Use this slender finger of rock as a landmark as you climb up talus slopes, then, just below the summit, traverse left across a steep slope to Milestone Pass (13,000'). This traverse is pretty spooky because it skirts the top of a big cliff and can be icy. From the pass, a wonderful descent brings you down Milestone Bowl to the creek (11,200') below Colby Pass.

The route then tackles the next pass, which is more of a steep ridge crossing. Climb very steeply above cliffs to the summit of the prominent ridge (12,000') trending south from Colby Pass. The views south are dominated by the imposing Kaweah peaks, especially the dark mass of Black Kaweah. The route then takes a long traverse above the headwaters of Kaweah River to Triple Divide Pass (12,200'), crossing into Kings Canyon National Park just north of Triple Divide Peak. If avalanche danger is high, it's better to skip the traverse and drop down to the river before climbing back up toward Triple Divide Pass.

From the pass, another great downhill run takes you west to Glacier Lake (11,650'). A very steep traverse leads south around to the head of Cloud Canyon, passing just below Lion Lake Pass. Staying on the Cloud Canyon side of the divide, make a long, sweeping traverse up the slope toward Glacier Divide. As you gain altitude, the peaks of Great Western Divide become visible over the prominent spine of The Whaleback. A short, steep climb accesses the top of the ridge just north of its junction with the main crest at Coppermine Pass (12,100'). Although the ridge is very exposed, camping on the spectacular ridge is highly recommended.

A short, steep gully on the west side of the pass brings you down into the equally sublime Deadman Canyon (11,600'). A slightly downhill traverse below Elizabeth Pass takes you to the obviously named Fin Pass (11,300') and back into Sequoia Park at Lonely Lake (10,800'). Spectacular views to

Looking back at Triple Divide Peak and Cloud Canyon.

Deadman Canyon from Glacier Ridge. DION GOLDSWORTHY PHOTO

the south, including the tops of Angel Wings and Hamilton Dome, accompany the route as it crosses over a low ridge (11,200') into the head of Buck Canyon.

A convoluted traverse finally brings you to The Tablelands (11,000') and the long, remarkable downhill run to Pear Lake Hut (9,200'). The hut, which is manned by winter rangers, is available for overnight stays with advance reservations. The route out from the hut is marked and skirts the slabs near Aster and Heather lakes before climbing over The Hump (9,400'), dropping down through the trees, and following Wolverton Creek to the trailhead at Wolverton Ski Area (7,300'). For an even more memorable ending, follow the marked ski trail over the ridge and down through the awe-inspiring giant sequoias to Giant Forest.

I Monarch Divide

Highlights:	Perhaps the ultimate backcountry ski tour.
Difficulty:	Class 3-4
Distance:	About 50 miles
Trailheads:	Roads End and Glacier Lodge
USGS 15′ Maps:	Marion Peak, Mount Pinchot, Mount Goddard, Big Pine
USGS 7.5′ Maps:	The Sphinx, Marion Peak, Mount Pinchot, Split Mountain

Monarch Divide

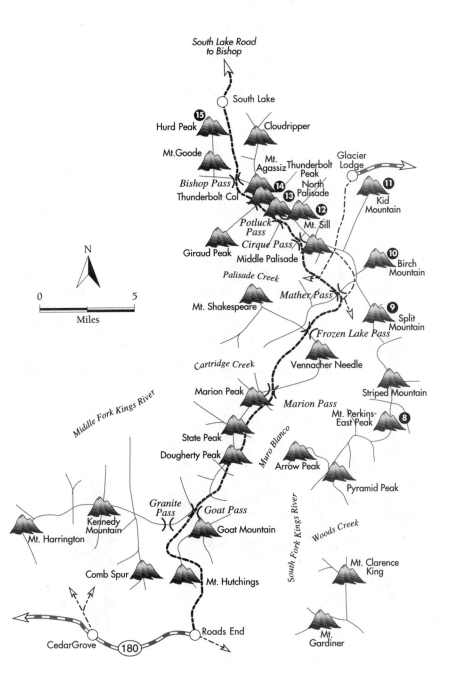

South Lake Road to Bishop

South Lake

15 Hurd Peak

Cloudripper

Mt. Goode

Mt. Agassiz

Thunderbolt Peak

Glacier Lodge

Bishop Pass

14 North Palisade

11 Kid Mountain

Thunderbolt Col

13

12 Mt. Sill

Potluck Pass

Cirque Pass

Giraud Peak

Middle Palisade

10 Birch Mountain

Palisade Creek

Mt. Shakespeare

Mather Pass

9 Split Mountain

Frozen Lake Pass

Cartridge Creek

Vennacher Needle

Striped Mountain

Marion Peak

Marion Pass

Mt. Perkins-East Peak

8

State Peak

Muro Blanco

Dougherty Peak

Arrow Peak

Pyramid Peak

Middle Fork Kings River

Granite Pass

Goat Pass

Kennedy Mountain

Goat Mountain

Woods Creek

Mt. Harrington

South Fork Kings River

Mt. Clarence King

Comb Spur

Mt. Hutchings

Cedar Grove

180

Roads End

Mt. Gardiner

N

0   5

Miles

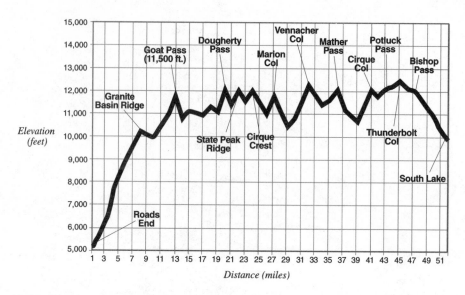

Elevation (feet)

Distance (miles)

Granite Basin Ridge

Goat Pass (11,500 ft.)

Dougherty Pass

Marion Col

Vennacher Col

Mather Pass

Potluck Pass

Cirque Col

Bishop Pass

State Peak Ridge

Cirque Crest

Thunderbolt Col

South Lake

Roads End

Overview: This tour should really be called the Cirque Crest Tour because it barely touches the Monarch Divide. This very regal tour is characterized by a series of wonderful traverses linking the great cirques along the ridge. The summit of Monarch Divide/Cirque Crest rises 6,000 feet above the South Fork and the Middle Fork of Kings River, and all along the route, there are fantastic views into those deep canyons and of Sierra Crest to the east. To top it off, there is also an abundance of great bowl skiing and peak descents along the way, and the tour through The Palisades provides a spectacular

Descending the north slope of Dougherty Peak.

finish. In many ways, this tour is as fine as the Sierra High Route, and some folks think it might be even better. You can obviously go east to west, or west to east. The route is described west to east for those folks who may choose to ski back to the east side on this route following a traverse of the High Route.

Route: It is possible to start this tour at Lewis Creek or Deer Cove and access the Monarch Divide at Mount Harrington, but the terrain and snow conditions usually don't warrant the extra effort. Anyway, the really fine skiing begins at Granite Basin. Our route starts at Roads End (5,000') in Kings Canyon and follows Copper Creek Trail up to Upper Tent Meadows (8,400'). The scenery just keeps getting better the higher you go. From the meadows, follow the trail over the low saddle (10,300') and enjoy great views south toward the Kings-Kern Divide and the High Route as you cross over a forested saddle and drop into Granite Basin (10,000').

From the middle of the basin, follow the creek draining the west side of Goat Mountain before making the easy climb to Goat Pass (11,450') and crossing Goat Crest. This pass leads you down to the upper Glacier Lakes (10,650'), back up to the low saddle (11,250') on the east side of the cirque, and then down to the lakes (10,900') on the North Fork of Kid Creek.

The route stays high on the east side of Cirque Crest, traversing above the deep canyon of the South Fork of Kings River, and includes spectacular views of Muro Blanco and the great mass of Arrow Peak to the east. Climb up the great south-facing bowl, then proceed directly over the summit of Dougherty Peak (12,241') before making the fine descent down the north slopes to the lakes (11,300') at the base of State Peak. After crossing the lakes, the route climbs the east bowl of State Peak and drops steeply off the north side of the east ridge (12,000') down to the lake basin (11,500') below.

Crossing the steep ridge (11,950') to the east drops you into the prominent valley on the south side of Marion Peak. When you reach the lakes (11,000') at the foot of the peak, turn north and follow the drainage to Marion Pass (12,100') east of the summit. The east slope of Marion Peak (12,719) provides an excellent ski run after a lunch stop atop the pass.

From the pass, there are great views down Cartridge Creek to Middle Fork Canyon, with Devils Crags and Black Divide forming a dramatic backdrop. The route makes a marvelous descent down below a huge rock tower to Marion Lake (10,300') before swinging around a V-shaped lake (10,650') and climbing up into the open, rolling terrain of Lake Basin (11,050'). From the basin, follow Cartridge Creek to its head at the lakes (11,500') on the west side of Vennacher Needle, then climb to Frozen Lake Pass (12,400') just west of a small pyramid peak.

The slopes leading down from the pass provide a great run to the head of huge Upper Basin (11,500'). Looming to the east is the massive hulk of Split Mountain. If conditions are right, the north slopes of Split Mountain (14,058') provide an excellent descent. From the head of Upper Basin, climb the steep slope to Mather Pass (12,100'), which may be topped a large cornice. From the pass, a fine descent leads down to Palisade Lakes perched at the head of

Above Muro Blanco on the Monarch Divide.

Looking south from The Palisades. VERN CLEVENGER PHOTO

deep LeConte Canyon. It is possible to escape the route by using very steep Southfork Pass to access the south fork of Big Pine Canyon and ultimately the trailhead at Glacier Lodge.

The route now traverses the very spectacular western escarpment of The Palisades. From the west end of Palisade Lakes, contour up and around to Cirque Pass (12,100'). Drop down to Glacier Creek before making the steep climb up ledges to Potluck Pass (12,150'). From here, the route stays very close to the sheer west faces of North Palisade and Thunderbolt Peak to reach Thunderbolt Col (12,400'). A slight downward traverse then leads to Bishop Pass (11,950'), where a final steep slope begins the fine run down the forested basin of the south fork of Bishop Creek to the trailhead at South Lake (9,750').

J Yosemite Border Tour

Highlights: Excellent skiing through a rarely visited section of
Yosemite National Park.

Difficulty: Class 3

Distance: About 45 miles

Trailheads: Rush Creek and Badger Pass

USGS 15' Maps: Devils Postpile, Tuolumne Meadows, Merced Peak,
Yosemite

USGS 7.5' Maps: June Lake, Mount Ritter, Mount Lyell, Merced Peak,
Sing Park, Half Dome

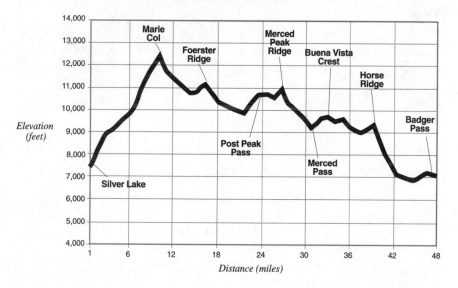

Overview: This tour is also known as the Yosemite High Route, and it rivals
the Sierra High Route as one of the area's best ski tours. It certainly has
everything—outrageous scenery, excellent skiing, a number of challenging
alternatives, and some truly fine peaks for ski descents. This tour is also
well-suited to lighter-weight equipment and has been done very quickly by
fit individuals using high-tech skating equipment.

The route has many things in common with the Sierra High Route. It
follows a natural boundary, which also serves as a border of a national park;
it weaves its way along the top of the divide separating two major rivers (the
Merced and the San Joaquin), and it finishes with an optional stay at a hut
(Ostrander) and a great descent through open forests to a ski area (Badger
Pass). This tour is not as populated, nor as technical, as its southern rival;
however, the remoteness and length of the tour definitely make it a serious
adventure that should not be taken lightly.

Yosemite Border Tour

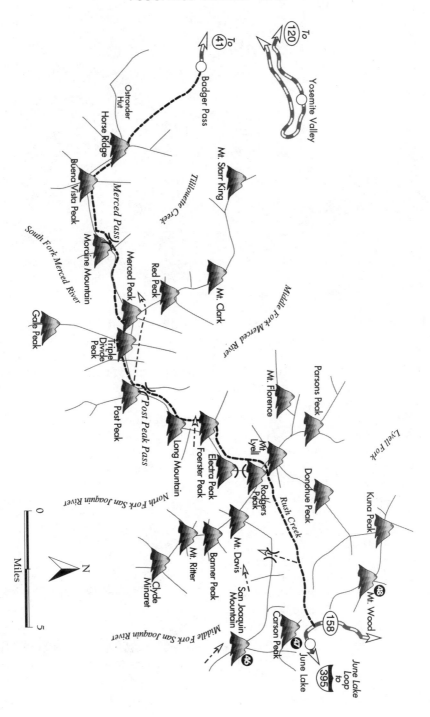

Touring in the headwaters of the Merced River. VERN CLEVENGER PHOTO

Route: The tour begins along the June Lake Loop near Silver Lake (7,300′) and follows Rush Creek up either the summer trail or the steep tramway to Gem Lake (9,050′). From here, follow the creek past Waugh Lake (9,450′) and up to Marie Lakes (10,850′). From the uppermost lake (11,200′), climb the small glacier and onto the steep pass (12,500′), crossing the southeast ridge of Mount Lyell.

From Mount Lyell, the route drops down the Lyell Fork of the Merced River past the large lake (11,300′) just west of Rodgers Peak. Follow the classic stairstep lakes below to the inlet of the lowest lake (10,200′) just northwest of Mount Ansel Adams. Then cross the steep north spur (11,200′) of Foerster Peak before traversing around the west side of the mountain to the lake (10,900′) at the head of Foerster Creek. A great downhill run leads to Harriet Lake (10,250′) below Long Mountain.

It is possible to reach this point from Mammoth Mountain via Thousand Island Lake (9,800′), then across the Ritter Range at North Glacier Pass (11,150′) and Lake Catherine (11,050′). A tricky contour drops through the headwaters

Moonset over the west side of The Minarets.
VERN CLEVENGER PHOTO

of the North Fork of the San Joaquin and across to the Twin Island Lakes (9,800'). From here, follow beautiful Bench Canyon past Blue Lake (10,500'), crossing the low ridge to the west (11,300') and dropping down to Harriet Lake.

From the lake, follow the obvious bench system above the Triple Peak Fork until just west of Isberg Peak, then turn south for the climb to Post Peak Pass (10,800'). From the

The Clark Range from Buena Vista Crest.
VERN CLEVENGER PHOTO

pass, follow the ridge above Post Lakes and around the north side of a small peak before heading down to Walton Lake (10,400'). Cross the south ridge of Triple Divide Peak at the obvious saddle (10,800') and contour around to the crossing (11,100') of the south ridge of Merced Peak. The upper section of Illilouette Creek provides a great ski down to Upper Merced Pass Lake (9,000'), where a short climb back up brings you to Merced Pass (9,300').

Depending on snow conditions, you might want to contour along the north or south side of the Buena Vista Crest; either route offers easy touring. Stay north of Buena Vista Peak, crossing over Horse Ridge (9,400') before descending to the hut at Ostrander Lake (8,500'). From the hut, there are a variety of marked trails out to Glacier Point Road. The most straightforward way is to follow Horizon Ridge down to Mono Meadow (6,800'). A gentle ski along the road quickly brings you to Badger Pass Ski Area (7,400'). During the winter, shuttle buses run on a regular schedule from the ski area to the valley floor.

K Mammoth to Yosemite

Highlights:	The most popular Sierra ski tour.
Difficulty:	Class 3
Distance:	About 50 miles
Trailheads:	Mammoth Mountain and Yosemite Valley
USGS 15' Maps:	Devils Postpile, Mono Craters, Tuolumne Meadows, Yosemite
USGS 7.5' Maps:	Mammoth Mountain, Mount Ritter, Koip Peak, Vogelsang Peak, Tioga Pass, Tenaya Lake, Yosemite Falls

Mammoth to Yosemite

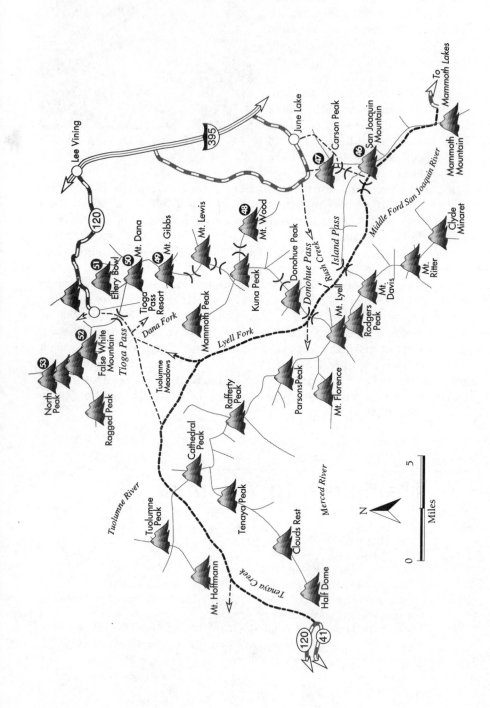

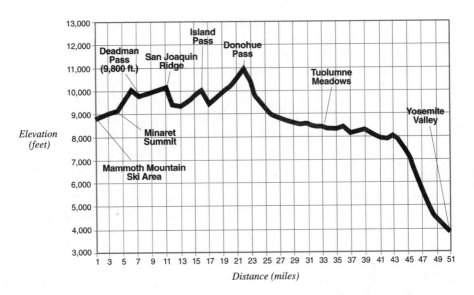

Elevation (feet)

Distance (miles)

Overview: The trans-Sierra tour from Mammoth to Yosemite Valley is probably the most popular backcountry tour in the Sierra and it's easy to understand why. The skiing terrain is remarkably moderate as the route winds its way past the spectacular Minarets into Yosemite National Park, making an easy crossing of the crest at Donohue Pass. The tour down Lyell Canyon and below the granite domes of Tuolumne Meadows is classic Nordic terrain. You follow the summer Tioga Pass Road past Tenaya Lake to the head of Snow Creek and the forested slopes leading to the rim of the incomparable Yosemite Valley. A final descent down the switchbacks of Snow Creek brings you to the valley floor.

There are many options for tours in the Yosemite high country. The easiest is the traverse of California 120 from Lee Vining over Tioga Pass through Tuolumne Meadows to Crane Flat or Yosemite Valley. The Tuolumne Meadows area is a great place for a base camp, with a winterized ski hut maintained by the park service and with rangers on duty all winter.

Route: This tour begins at Mammoth Mountain Ski Area (9,000'), and after a short jaunt west to Minaret Summit (9,200'), the route begins heading north along the San Joaquin Ridge. This windswept ridge is a notoriously bad spot to be caught in a whiteout, and be careful of the monstrous cornices that form along the ridge in the vicinity of Deadman Pass (9,800'). Stay well back from the edge here.

From the pass, the route parallels the Pacific Crest Trail (PCT) along a shelf on the west side of the ridge below the summits of Two Teats and San Joaquin Mountain. The route finally drops down to the bench at the junction with Agnew Pass Trail (9,900'). This pass provides an escape route to lower Rush Creek and the June Lake Loop. From just below Agnew Pass, follow the PCT across the head of the San Joaquin River Canyon to the east end of beautiful Thousand Island Lake (9,800'). There are many good campsites on the north side of the lake, and the views of Banner Peak and Mount Ritter are truly breathtaking.

From the lake, the route follows the PCT over the low saddle of Island Pass (10,250') and makes a delightful descent into the drainage of Rush Creek. After crossing the forks of Rush Creek (9,650'), head up gentle slopes to Donohue Pass (11,050') and the border of Yosemite National Park. A short, steep pitch followed by another wonderful descent brings you to the floor of Lyell Canyon (9,600'), where a long, flat ski through the meadows along the Lyell Fork of the Tuolumne River eventually leads to the ranger station at Tuolumne Meadows (8,600'). This section can be very wet and may take longer than expected.

From Tuolumne Meadows, the route follows snowbound California 120 as it weaves through the world-famous domes and along the shore of Tenaya Lake (8,150'). Beyond the lake, the road traverses potentially dangerous slabs as it climbs to Olmstead Point (8,400'). A better route follows the creek below the road. Join the road again at Olmstead Point and follow it to Snow Creek Trail, which leads to the valley rim (6,700') just east of Washington Column. The views of Half Dome and Yosemite Valley make a fantastic climax to your tour as you wind down the switchbacks past booming Snow Creek Falls to the valley floor (4,000').

If you are heading back to the east side of the range, you may prefer to follow the crest route as it traverses east from the top of Donohue Pass past Blacktop and Kuna peaks, topping out at Kuna Pass (11,800') and dropping down to Helen Lake (10,950'). From Helen Lake, a delightful run brings you out to Dana Meadows (9,600'), then up to Tioga Pass (9,945'). After a short

San Joaquin Ridge and Donohue Pass.

Crossing Donohue Pass. DION GOLDSWORTHY PHOTO

drop down the east side, you reach Tioga Pass Resort (9,550'), where the road may be plowed. You can also use Mono Pass (10,700').

As previously noted, the easiest trans-Sierra tour follows California 120 over Tioga Pass from Lee Vining to Tuolumne Meadows and on to Crane Flat (6,200') or Yosemite Valley. This route is the fastest way to cross the Sierra in the winter and can be done in a long day. It is regularly used as a route back to the east side after finishing one of the other trans-Sierra tours.

Selected Short Tours

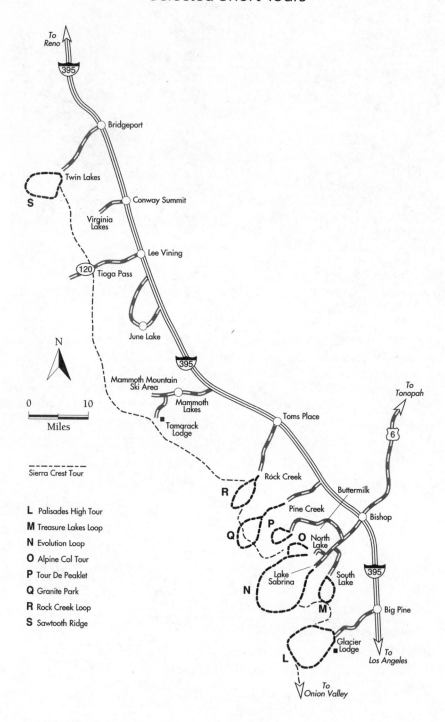

Sierra Crest Tour

L Palisades High Tour
M Treasure Lakes Loop
N Evolution Loop
O Alpine Col Tour
P Tour De Peaklet
Q Granite Park
R Rock Creek Loop
S Sawtooth Ridge

SELECTED SHORT TOURS

Some of the finest tours in the Sierra don't really go anywhere at all. Some head a few miles into a base camp with spectacular views or excellent bowl skiing. Others traverse around a peak standing in the center of an open drainage or head straight to the base of a fine ski descent. The bottom line is that you don't need to travel all the way across the Sierra to see wonderful country or to find really good skiing. These short tours offer the best balance between wilderness travel and excellent skiing. You don't have to carry nearly as much gear, trudge as far, or travel so conservatively.

These shorter tours make great weekend trips, but they can also be stretched into longer and more relaxed adventures. For most folks, these tours are the best introduction to skiing the High Sierra. First, every tour starts and ends at the same place, making logistics easy. Secondly, high daily mileage isn't a big concern so you can carry more luxuries. Best of all, you don't need to feel guilty about lingering in a fine area because you don't always need to be "getting on down the trail." On these tours, you're already there.

Short spring tours and base camps have long been a Sierra tradition. This combination is a great way to gain the experience needed for longer tours. The classic *Sierra Club Manual of Ski Mountaineering* was written mainly about a trip into the head of Rock Creek Canyon in 1940. Extreme skiers and boarders will be drawn to areas like The Palisades, Lamarck Col, and Sawtooth Ridge because these locations have an abundance of steep and challenging descents, but these shorter tours still require a degree of caution and self-sufficiency in order to maintain a margin of safety. The selections I've detailed here are really just the tip of the iceberg—just an introduction to the endless number of possibilities available in the range.

Touring in Rock Creek Canyon.

L Palisades High Tour

Highlights:	Visits some of the most spectacular alpine terrain in the range.
Difficulty:	Class 3-4
Distance:	About 20 miles
Trailhead:	Glacier Lodge
USGS 7.5′ Maps:	Split Mountain, North Palisade, Coyote Flat, Mount Thompson

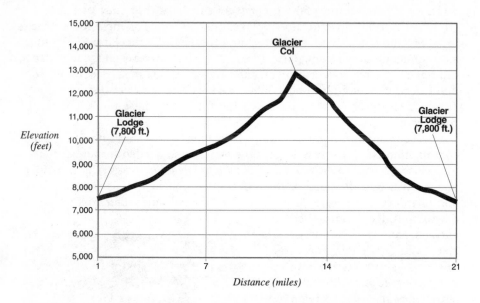

Overview: The Palisades, the most alpine region in California, is home to the largest glaciers in the Sierra. The peaks are world-famous for their mountaineering challenges and their difficult ski descents. This tour provides a unique view of the north and south forks of Big Pine Creek. The first-class ski descents in The Palisades include the U-Notch, V-Notch, and the Underhill Couloirs. This is an excellent ski mountaineering route requiring basic climbing skills and good mountain sense.

Temple Crag and The Palisades.

Route: The tour begins at Glacier Lodge (7,800′) and follows the North Fork of Big Pine Creek past First Falls and into the shallow basin below Second Falls (8,500′). The sandy slopes above lead to Lon Chaney's old stone cabin in the delightful Cienega Mirth (9,200′).

Palisades High Tour

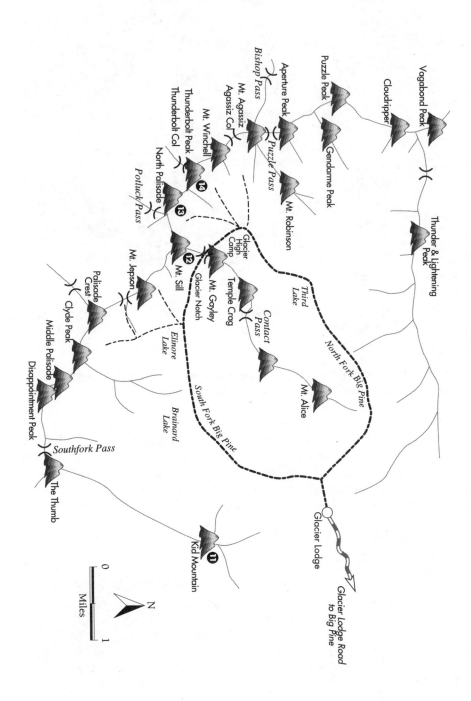

Palisades Glacier from Mount Agassiz.

Enjoy the view of the dark towers of Temple Crag as you make the gentle climb through sparse timber following the creek up to First Lake (10,000'). Pass high above Second Lake before arriving at stunning Third Lake (10,250') at the foot of Temple Crag.

From the lake, don't follow the summer trail, but rather climb the steep gully to the west below the imposing north faces of Temple Crag and Mount Gayley to reach a camp on the terminal moraine of the Palisade Glacier (12,150'). There are a number of obvious skiing challenges here. Perched above the gaping bergschrund of the glacier, lie the Northeast Couloir of Mount Sill (14,162'), the V-Notch, the U-Notch, Clyde Couloir of North Palisade (14,242'), and the Underhill Couloirs of Thunderbolt Peak (14,003'). Around the prominent cleaver to the north, the north and northeast couloirs of Thunderbolt lie above Thunderbolt Glacier, as well as the gullies on Mount Winchell (13,775') and Mount Agassiz (13,893').

Ascend the eastern edge of the glacier to the bergschrund. Cross the 'schrund and climb steep snow above to reach Glacier Notch (13,050'). The obvious L-shaped couloir of Mount Sill lies just above the pass between the prominent Swiss Arête and the subsidiary summit of Apex Peak to the north. From Glacier Notch, drop onto Sill Glacier (12,800') below the sheer east

High camp on Palisades Traverse.
GORDON WILTSIE PHOTO

face of Mount Sill before making the great run down the bowl to Elinore Lake (11,000'). The impressive north face of Clyde Peak, with its twin north couloirs and prominent rock arêtes, lies directly to the south. The route onto Middle Palisade Glacier is blocked by the wall of the northeast ridge of Clyde. Our route heads east down the drainage to join the route from Contact Pass at Willow Lake (9,600'), then follows the summer trail out the South Fork of Big Pine Creek and back to Glacier Lodge. The side trip up to Finger Lake and Middle Palisade Glacier is worthwhile.

M   Treasure Lakes Loop

Highlights: A popular tour offering excellent skiing with plenty of opportunities for ski descents.
Difficulty: Class 2-3
Distance: About 10 miles
Trailhead: South Lake
USGS 7.5' Maps: Mount Thompson, North Palisade

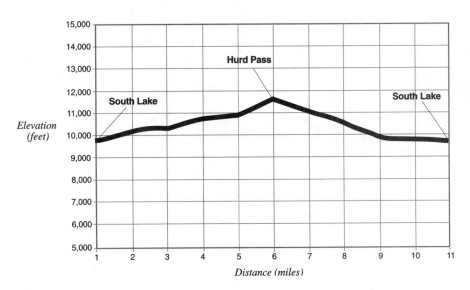

Overview: This delightful tour links the spectacular headwaters of the South Fork of Bishop Creek, visits Bishop Pass and Treasure Lakes areas, and circles the impressive pyramid of Hurd Peak. There are many excellent day tour possibilities, including skiing over Bishop Pass into scenic Dusy Basin at the western edge of The Palisades and touring up into the alpine cirque at the base of Mount Thompson. There is also some outrageous bowl skiing in the area, as well as the fine ski descents of Mount Goode, Mount Johnson, Mount, Gilbert, and Mount Thompson.

Treasure Lakes Loop

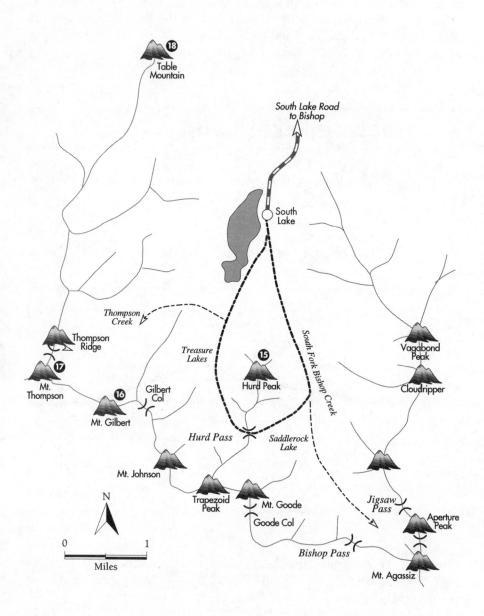

Table Mountain **18**

South Lake Road to Bishop

South Lake

Thompson Creek

Thompson Ridge

Mt. Thompson **17**

Mt. Gilbert **16**

Gilbert Col

Treasure Lakes

Hurd Peak **15**

South Fork Bishop Creek

Vagabond Peak

Cloudripper

Hurd Pass

Saddlerock Lake

Mt. Johnson

N

Trapezoid Peak

Mt. Goode

Goode Col

Jigsaw Pass

Aperture Peak

0   1
Miles

Bishop Pass

Mt. Agassiz

Route: From the dam at South Lake (9,750'), follow the summer trail to the bench above the lake, then follow the small valley draining Long Lake (10,750'). The sheer north face of Mount Goode beckons from the south as you skirt the east side of Hurd Peak on a gentle climb to Margaret Lake (10,950'). If your goal is to make a ski descent of Mount Goode (13,085') or detour over Bishop Pass into Dusy Basin, you might want to make a base camp in the last sheltering trees at Saddlerock Lake (11,100').

Our route, however, contours west from Margaret Lake to the low saddle of Hurd Col (11,750'). The rocky mountain just to the south is known as Trapezoid Peak. From the pass, you can look down into the basin holding the Treasure Lakes. A moderately steep drop leads you to the uppermost of these lakes (11,175'). The wonderful bowls below Mount Johnson (12,868') are worth exploring from here before continuing down to the largest lake (10,650').

This lake makes a great base camp for ski descents of Mount Johnson and Mount Gilbert (13,106'), as well as the bowls below the peaks. As a day tour, you can cross the steep ridge to the west to access the glacier on the north side of Mount Gilbert and Mount Thompson. This area feels like a scaled-down version of The Palisades, and there are a number of very challenging couloirs that can be skied from the summit ridge of Mount Thompson (13,494'). Less challenging, but no less attractive, is the fine east slope of the high point of Thompson Ridge (13,323'), which is also known as Ski Mountaineers Peak.

From Treasure Lakes, follow the creek drainage north down open slopes towards South Lake. Just above the lake, the forest becomes very dense, and difficult rock benches guard the route out onto the drained lakebed. Once

Looking south over Gilbert/Thompson Cirque.

Skiing the lower slopes of Mount Gilbert.

you reach the lake, a short tour around its shores quickly brings you back to the trailhead. Be careful skiing on the ice of the lake because it is often dangerously thin.

N   Evolution Loop

Highlights: A less challenging version of a Sierra Crest tour.
Difficulty: Class 3
Distance: About 30 miles
Trailhead: Lake Sabrina
USGS 7.5′ Maps: Mount Thompson, Mount Goddard, Mount Darwin

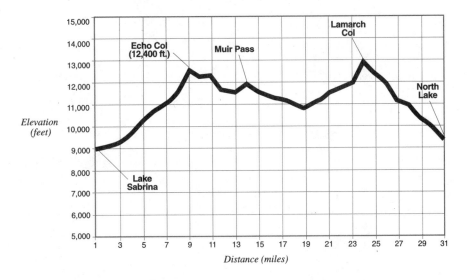

Elevation (feet) vs *Distance (miles)* elevation profile showing: Lake Sabrina, Echo Col (12,400 ft.), Muir Pass, Lamarch Col, North Lake.

Overview: This is a shortened version of the popular summer route over Muir Pass from South Lake to North Lake. The popular tour over Echo Col to Muir Hut is a very valid tour in its own right, providing easy access to the heart of the High Sierra and the remote Ionian Basin. From Muir Pass, the tour makes a delightful descent through Evolution Basin before climbing back out through spectacular Darwin Canyon and returning to the east side over Lamarck Col. Along the way, there are a number of fine ski descents, including Black Giant, Mount Theodore Solomons, and the north face of Mount Darwin. Or, you may just

Touring up to Echo Col.

87

Evolution Loop

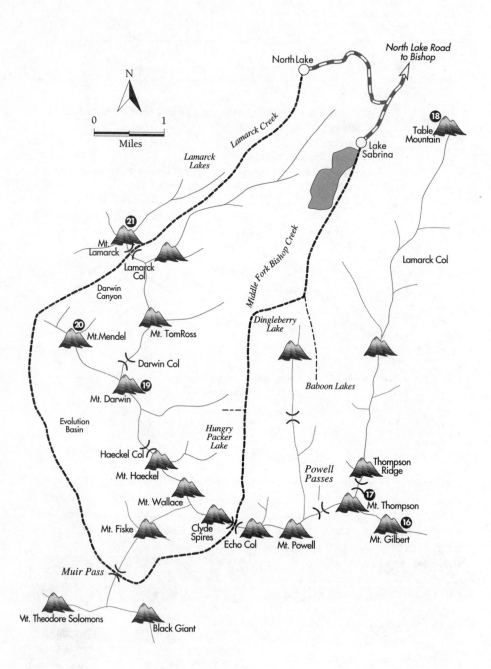

want to base camp at Hungry Packer Lake and explore the wonderful bowls on the east side of the Evolution group.

Route: This tour begins at the dam at Lake Sabrina (9,150') and immediately abandons the summer trail. After skiing around the drained lakeshore, follow the drainage of Bishop Creek as it climbs up benches to beautiful Blue Lake (10,400'). From here, you can ski south up the valley past Baboon Lakes (11,000') to Sunset Lake (11,500') and the Thompson/Powell Glacier. The northeast couloir of Mount Powell offers a fine descent. You can even link up with the main route by skiing over the ridge trending north from Mount Powell (11,900') and dropping down the very steep slopes to Moonlight Lake (11,050').

The main route, however, heads west from Blue Lake below a prominent unnamed spire and around to Dingleberry Lake (10,500'). Follow the drainage south toward the great rock face of Picture Peak presiding over Hungry Packer and Moonlight lakes (11,050'). From Moonlight Lake, the route climbs into the great cirque holding Echo Lake (11,600') before making the final climb below Clyde Spires to Echo Col (12,400'). A steep descent takes you past the lake below (11,500') and down to the John Muir Trail (11,000'), then a climb brings you back up to Helen Lake (11,600').

Turn west and climb to the stone shelter sitting atop Muir Pass (11,950'). This hut makes a sheltered (although a bit chilly) base for ski descents of the surrounding peaks, including Mount Theodore Solomons (13,034') and Black Giant (13,330'). A fine detour from the pass leads past Black Giant into

Touring in the Evolution Basin. JIM STIMSON PHOTO

The Muir Hut.

Ionian Basin. From Muir Pass, a wonderful descent through Evolution Basin takes you past Wanda Lake (11,400′) and Sapphire Lake (11,000′) before reaching beautiful Evolution Lake (10,850′). Climb north onto the Darwin Bench (11,200′) before contouring into classic, U-shaped Darwin Canyon (11,600′) to the east. From the uppermost lakes (12,100′), the great north face of Mount Darwin (13,831′) provides a very challenging ski descent.

The main route crosses the crest about one-half mile farther north at Lamarck Col (12,900′), just south of the summit of Mount Lamarck (13,417′). Make sure you pick the right saddle. The descent from Lamarck Col is a classic, following the broad valley to the northeast before dropping down the steep slopes to Upper Darwin Lake (10,900′). This lake makes a great base camp for skiing the challenging couloirs of Mount Lamarck and Keyhole Plateau. From the lake, follow Lamarck Creek past Lower Lamarck Lake (10,650′) and down steep, forested slopes to Grass Lake (9,900′), then follow the summer trail down to North Lake (9,400′) and back to Lake Sabrina via the road.

O   Alpine Col Tour

Highlights: A fine loop into the heart of the range, long appreciated by ski mountaineers.
Difficulty: Class 3
Distance: About 20 miles
Trailhead: North Lake
USGS 7.5′ Maps: Mount Darwin

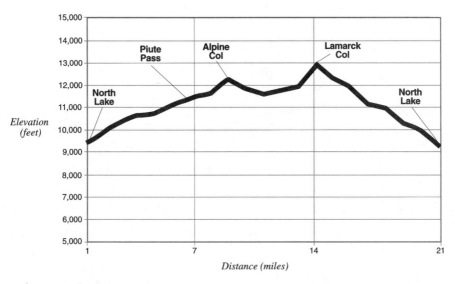

Overview: This is another excellent short tour that crosses the crest into the high country of Kings Canyon National Park. The tour follows the moderate route over Piute Pass before crossing the Glacier Divide at Alpine Col and dropping down into spectacular Darwin Canyon. Layover days will allow you to explore beautiful Evolution Basin, as well as to make ski descents of Mount Darwin, Mount Lamarck, Mount Humphreys, and other fine peaks in the area. This is a perfect shakedown trip for folks looking to try a longer, more difficult tour like the Sierra High Route or the Monarch Divide.

Route: The tour begins at North Lake (9,400) and climbs the summer route up the North Fork of Bishop Creek below colorful Piute Crags. A steep traverse through a short cliff band leads to Loch Leven (10,750′) and the broad valley above, which you follow past Piute

Camp below the Glacier Divide.

Alpine Col Tour

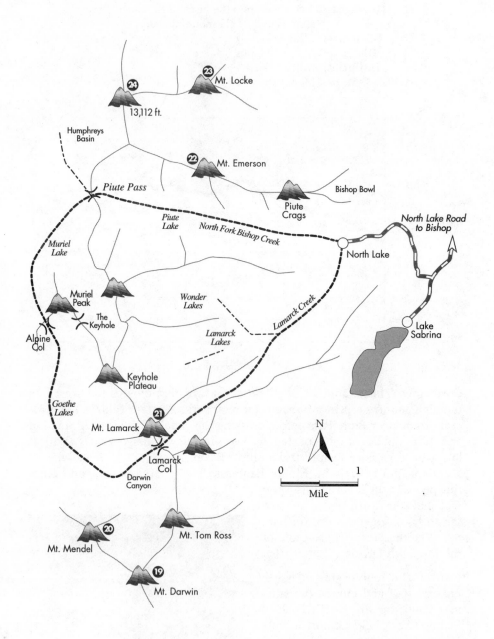

Mt. Locke

13,112 ft.

Humphreys Basin

Mt. Emerson

Bishop Bowl

Piute Pass

Piute Crags

Piute Lake

North Fork Bishop Creek

North Lake Road to Bishop

Muriel Lake

North Lake

Muriel Peak

Wonder Lakes

Lamarck Creek

The Keyhole

Lake Sabrina

Alpine Col

Lamarck Lakes

Keyhole Plateau

Goethe Lakes

Mt. Lamarck

N

Lamarck Col

0   1

Darwin Canyon

Mile

Mt. Mendel

Mt. Tom Ross

Mt. Darwin

Muriel Peak and The Keyhole.

Lake (10,950') to the final short climb to Piute Pass (11,425'). A great detour from the pass leads northwest into Humphreys Basin and Desolation Lake (11,375') below the broad bulk of Mount Humphreys.

From Piute Pass, the route heads southwest around Muriel Lake (10,350') and on to Goethe Lake (11,550') in the stunning Goethe Cirque. Directly ahead is the sheer north face of Mount Goethe rising above the glacier. Climb steeply out of the cirque to Alpine Col (12,350') just southwest of Muriel Peak. From the col, the impressive north faces of Mount Darwin and Mount Mendel loom over rugged Darwin Canyon.

Drop down a steep bowl to the large lake below (11,900'), ski past the lake at the mouth of the cirque (11,550'), and contour east to the lakes of Darwin Canyon (11,600'). A base camp here allows you to explore Darwin Glacier, as well as make a ski descent of the great north slope of Mount Darwin (13,831') or contemplate Mendel Couloir. On the climb east to Lamarck Col (12,900'), be sure to take the saddle just south of Mount Lamarck (13,417')—not the obvious one near the small pyramid farther south, because that pass drops you down steep slopes into the wrong drainage.

Mount Lamarck and the Lamarck Col route. Vern Clevenger photo

From the top of the pass, follow the long, gentle valley to the northeast, then drop down a steep slope to Upper Lamarck Lake (10,900'). This lake can be used as a base camp for skiing the gullies of Mount Lamarck and Keyhole Plateau. From the lake, follow Lamarck Creek past Lower Lamarck Lake (10,650') and down the steep, forested slopes to Grass Lake (9,900'). Follow the summer trail from the lake down to the road at North Lake (9,400').

P Tour De Peaklet

Highlights: The easiest tour in this guidebook and a great introduction to the Sierra.
Difficulty: Class 3
Distance: About 10 miles
Trailhead: Buttermilk Road
USGS 7.5' Maps: Mount Tom

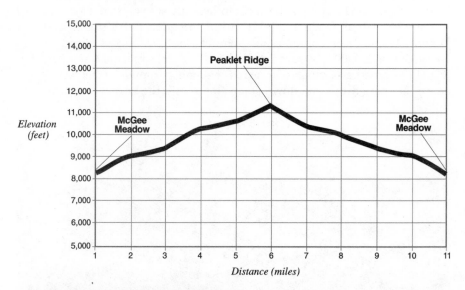

Overview: The Humphreys Glacier is pretty large by Sierra standards and there is a good-sized bergschrund at the juncture between the couloir and glacier. The north face of Mount Humphreys is one of the grand *nordwands* of the range. Therefore, even though this route is relatively short, it is very alpine in character and makes a great shakedown cruise for longer tours.

Mount Locke and Mount Humpheys.

94

Tour De Peaklet

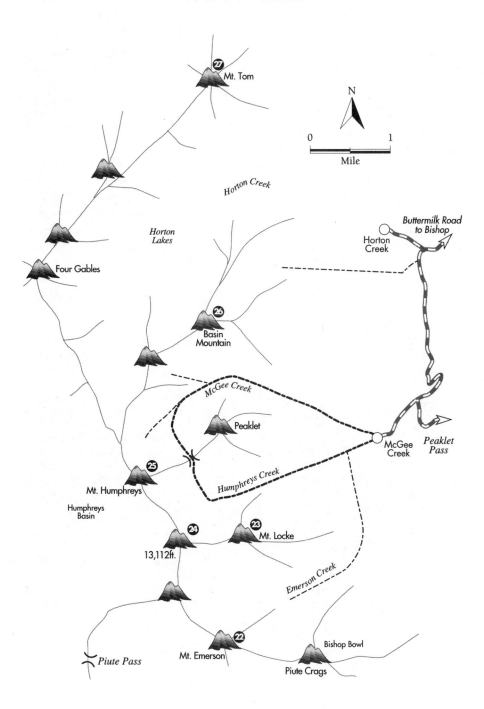

In fact, this has long been a favorite warm-up route of local guides before taking clients on longer tours. The pass between the forks of McGee Creek marks the start of the classic east ridge climb on Mount Humphreys. If you have the time, this is a highly recommended diversion.

Route: The towering bulk of Mount Humphreys dominates the view west from downtown Bishop. To get there, turn west on California 168 in the center of the town of Bishop and go west about 5 miles. Turn right onto the dirt Buttermilk Road, drive past the Peabody Boulders, and continue up into the high desert of the Buttermilk country (7,800'). About a mile past the turn for Basin Mountain, the road reaches a cattle guard and passes through a pretty meadow with aspen trees.

There are nice campsites at the crossing of McGee Creek (high-clearance vehicles recommended). Climb the moraine past the crossing and take the rough road on the right to another junction near a creek gauging station. The road is often not passable, even to four-wheel-drive vehicles, beyond this point. Follow the road or the creek up to the meadow (8,400') below Longley Reservoir. Follow McGee Creek around the impressive north face of Peaklet to reach the old reservoir (10,700').

From here, climb up onto the moraine and into the cirque below the sheer north face of Mount Humphreys. Turn south and follow the edge of the glacier before the final climb to the rocky saddle (11,700') between Peaklet and Mount Humphreys. The classic knife-edge climb of the east ridge of Mount Humphreys begins here, weaving around and over towers to the summit (13,986').

Looking up at the northeast face of Mount Humphreys.

From the pass, the colorful peak to the south (13,112') harbors the notorious ice climb/ski descent The Checkered Demon, as well as the more moderate Kindergarden Chute. Drop down the south side to the drainage below, following it east below the fine Wahoo Gullies of Mount Locke and eventually out to McGee Creek Road and the parking area.

Q Granite Park

Highlights: Moderate terrain combined with fine alpine views.
Difficulty: Class 2-3
Distance: About 30 miles
Trailhead: Pine Creek
USGS 7.5' Maps: Mount Tom, Mount Hilgard

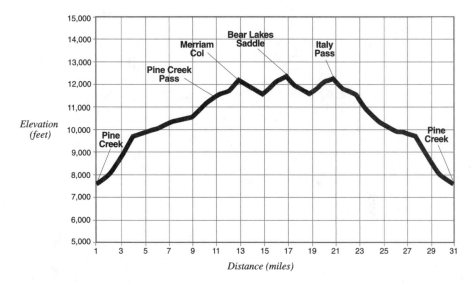

Overview: This tour takes in some of the finest high-country scenery in the Sierra. The colorful rock of lower Pine Creek Canyon contrasts brilliantly with the orange granite spires surrounding Granite Park and Royce Lakes. This tour also provides access to little-visited Bear Lakes below Seven Gables, as well as a side trip into the huge basin of Lake Italy. There is a fine base camp at Honeymoon Lake and the entrance to

Kimberly Walker touring up into Granite Park.

Granite Park

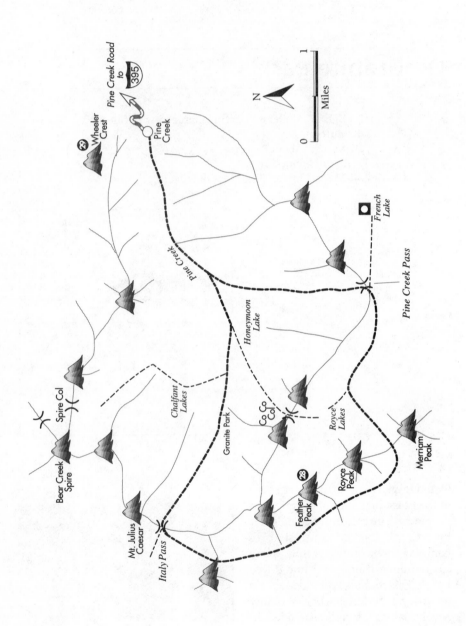

Camp in the Royce Lake Basin.

Granite Park. The drawback to this area, however, is that access is via very avalanche-prone Pine Creek Canyon.

Route: The tour begins at the summer trailhead in Pine Creek Canyon (7,500') below the still active tungsten mine and mill. To reach this trailhead, travel through Rovana on Pine Creek Road, just north of Bishop off US Highway 395. Be aware that the first few miles of the trip are major-league avalanche terrain. Follow the summer trail past the ruins of the Brownstone Mine (9,200'), before making an intimidating traverse to reach the wilderness boundary. The traverse eases before reaching Lower Pine Lake (9,950'). Follow the drainage past Upper Pine Lake (10,200'), and climb up the course of a gentle stream to the broad saddle of Pine Creek Pass (11,100').

From the pass, the route turns west and continues climbing moderately to the first of the Royce Lakes (11,650') at the base of the prominent north pillar of Merriam Peak. You may want to make a base camp at the largest of these lakes (11,725') and sample the fine bowl skiing here. Feather Peak (13,242') is also a fine objective, with a series of very challenging couloirs gracing its north and northwest faces.

Our route ascends the bowl (great skiing in its own right) between Merriam Peak (13,100') and Royce Peak (13,253'), both of which are easily climbed from the pass at its head (12,200'). Drop down the west side past a small lake (11,850') before heading west for the lakes (11,200') below La Salle Lake. A short, but steep, climb takes you to the pass (12,000') leading into Bear Lakes Basin, where the sheer eastern face of Seven Gables looms over the aptly named Vee Lake (11,150').

High camp on the west side of Feather Peak. VERN CLEVENGER PHOTO

Italy Pass and the Seven Gables. VERN CLEVENGER PHOTO

Climb north over benches, past upper Bear Lakes (11,700') before entering the hanging valley (12,150') just east of a prominent pyramid peak. From the northern end of this valley, a high traverse above Jumble Lake brings you to Italy Pass (12,300') at the foot of Mount Julius Caesar. From the pass, a wonderful descent takes you beneath the spectacular granite spires of upper Granite Park (11,600'). A nice side tour contours north to Chalfant Lakes and the impressive south face of Bear Creek Spire. The descent from Granite Park follows the drainage past Honeymoon Lake (10,400') and down to Upper Pine Lake before heading back out Pine Creek Canyon to the trailhead.

R Rock Creek Loop

Highlights: A little sample of everything that Rock Creek Canyon has to offer.
Difficulty: Class 3
Distance: About 20 miles
Trailhead: Rock Creek Lake
USGS 7.5' Maps: Mount Morgan, Mount Abbot

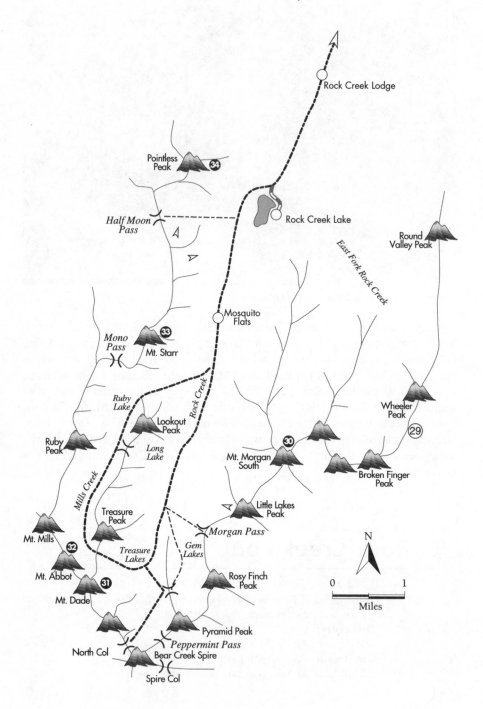

Rock Creek Loop

Rock Creek Lodge

Pointless Peak ㉞

Half Moon Pass

Rock Creek Lake

Round Valley Peak

East Fork Rock Creek

Mosquito Flats

Mono Pass

Mt. Starr ㉝

Ruby Lake

Rock Creek

Lookout Peak

Wheeler Peak

㉙

Ruby Peak

Long Lake

Mt. Morgan South

㉚

Broken Finger Peak

Mills Creek

Treasure Peak

Little Lakes Peak

Morgan Pass

Mt. Mills

㉜

Treasure Lakes

Gem Lakes

N

Mt. Abbot

Mt. Dade ㉛

Rosy Finch Peak

0   1

Miles

North Col

Pyramid Peak

Peppermint Pass

Bear Creek Spire

Spire Col

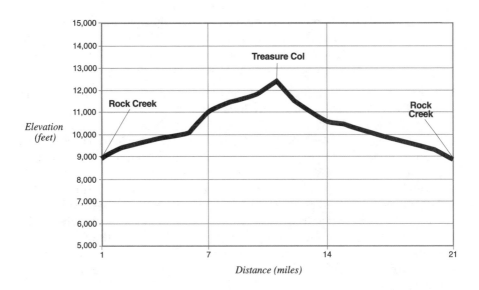

Overview: This canyon has long been considered one of the finest in the range for backcountry skiing. The flat floor of Little Lakes Valley offers excellent touring, while the high glacial cirques along the sides and at the head of the canyon offer spectacular bowls and couloirs. The trip around Treasure Peak samples the best that this beautiful canyon has to offer. In particular, Treasure Lakes is one of the best locations for a spring base camp in the eastern Sierra. There is a broad range of alternatives to explore in this scenic canyon. The tour around Mount Starr over Half Moon and Mono

Mount Abbot and upper Rock Creek Canyon.

103

passes is a great day trip for experienced skiers. Touring through the gentle terrain of the Tamarack Bench offers an entirely different view and experience from the main canyon. Meanwhile, Patricia Bowl, Half Moon Pass, and the north slope of Mount Morgan offer excellent powder skiing.

Route: The tour starts at the end of the plowed road (8,900') leading up the canyon from Toms Place on US Highway 395. Begin by following the summer road to Rock Creek Lake (9,700') below the massive avalanche gullies on the east side of Pointless Peak (12,252') and Mount Starr (12,832'). At Mosquito Flats (10,200'), leave the road and enter the classic, U-shaped canyon of Little Lakes Valley at Mack Lake (10,350').

From the meadow just beyond the lake, follow the stream draining Ruby Lake up a narrow, steep gully to reach a bench system leading to Ruby Lake (11,100'). The sheer granite cliffs of Ruby Wall serve as a spectacular backdrop for the lake. Contour around the east edge of the lake, then climb up a moderate slope to reach the upper drainage and Mills Lake (11,700'). Continue south up another moderately steep slope to the glacier at the base of Mount Abbot and Mount Mills (12,200').

The route continues by contouring east below the south slopes of Treasure Peak to reach the broad saddle (12,500') between Mount Dade and Treasure Peak. From the saddle, a long, steep descent leads down a shallow drainage at the base of Treasure Peak to the basin of Treasure Lakes (11,175') below. There are wonderful bowls in the upper cirque just above these lakes, and the hourglass-shaped couloir below the summit of Mount Dade (13,600') makes an excellent ski descent.

Touring up towards Mount Abbot from Ruby Lake.

High camp at Ruby Lake.

Dave Page skiing below Ruby Wall on Rock Creek Loop.

To finish the tour, turn north and drop down the moderately steep Treasure Lakes gully to reach the inlet to Long Lake (10,550'). Continue down the drainage, passing Box Lake, Heart Lake, and Marsh Lake before closing the loop back at Mack Lake. Follow the drainage back down to Mosquito Flats and the summer road past Rock Creek Lake to the parking area.

S Sawtooth Ridge

Highlights: A ski mountaineer's idea of heaven.
Difficulty: Class 3-4
Distance: About 20 miles
Trailhead: Twin Lakes
USGS 7.5′ Maps: Matterhorn Peak, Dunderberg Peak, Buckeye Ridge

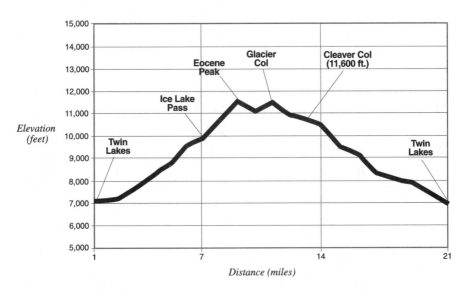

Overview: This route tours below the spectacular alpine terrain of Sawtooth Ridge. The rugged granite towers of the ridge provide an incredible backdrop for the route, culminating in dramatic Matterhorn Peak and the fantastic run down Horse Creek. This tour is tailor-made for the ski mountaineer who wants to combine some great climbing with excellent skiing. An easier introduction to the area follows the drainage up Cattle Creek, Turquoise Lake, and onto the glacier below the imposing north couloirs of Twin Peaks. A short traverse takes you over the low saddle to the west and down the great natural half-pipe of upper Horse Creek to the meadow below.

Route: This route begins at the Twin Lakes Campground (7,100′) on the west end of the lakes, southwest of the town of Bridgeport. Follow the gentle valley of Robinson Creek as it heads west and parallels Sawtooth Ridge. Just before the canyon closes off at Barney Lake, the route turns south and follows the creek draining Little Slide Canyon. After an initial steep section, the route eases

Sawtooth Ridge.

Sawtooth Ridge

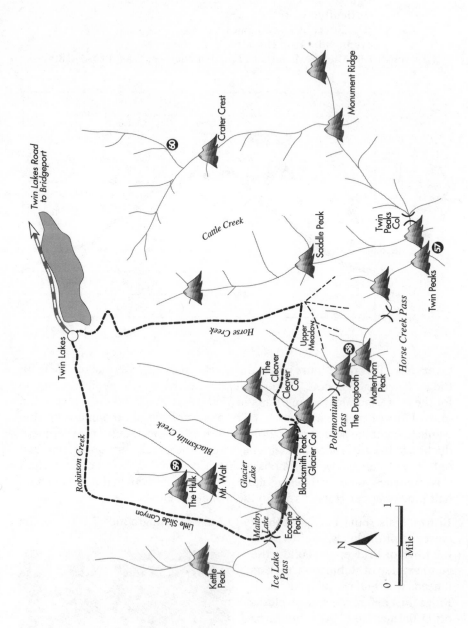

Touring on Sawtooth Glacier.

into the hanging valley above (8,000'). After another steep climb, the route levels off (9,600') below the spectacular granite ramparts of The Incredible Hulk and Kettle Peak. The route then ascends past Maltby Lake (9,800') to reach Ice Lake and Ice Lake Pass (10,000').

Once at the pass, don't stop climbing. Turn east and ascend the slopes to the summit of Eocene Peak (11,581). The peak marks the west end of Sawtooth Ridge and offers an excellent descent off the north side to Glacier Lake (10,100') and Blacksmith Creek. From the peak, traverse the south side of Blacksmith Peak to reach the notch of Glacier Col (11,600') between Blacksmith Peak and Cleaver Peak. A very steep drop leads north onto small Blacksmith Glacier (11,200'). From the glacier, cross The Cleaver at Cleaver Col (11,560') and access Sawtooth Glacier (11,200'). The next section traverses below the serrated ridgeline marked by The Sawblade and The Three Teeth. At the prominent rocky buttress of The Dragtooth, drop a few hundred feet to the small tarn (10,600') below Matterhorn Glacier.

From here, it is very easy to access the attractive couloirs and bowls surrounding Matterhorn Peak (12,264'), including the classic east couloir. At this point, you've probably had enough traversing and it's time to point your skis downhill for the fine run into the drainage of Horse Creek (8,300'). With any luck, you may be able to ski all the way back down to Twin Lakes. If you haven't had enough, you can traverse around to Horse Creek Pass (10,700') at the very head of the Horse Creek run and ride that drainage all the way down to the lake.

Classic Peak Descents

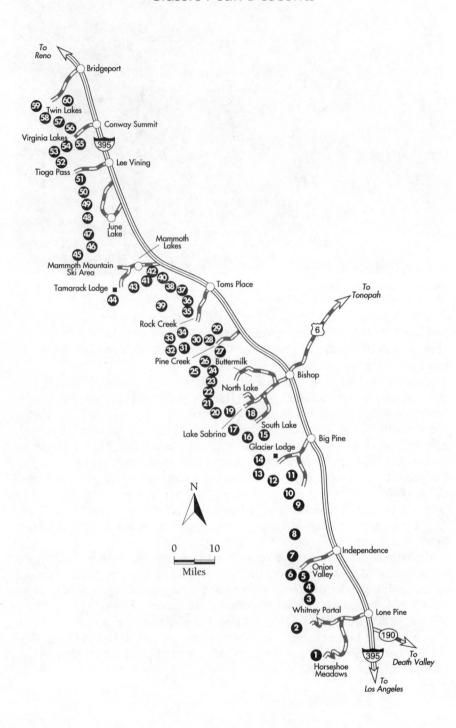

CLASSIC PEAK DESCENTS

The Sierra Nevada offers some of the best ski and snowboard descents anywhere. Sure, places like Crested Butte, Valdez, the Tetons, and the Wasatch have great terrain, but for sheer numbers of challenging couloirs and beautiful bowls, the Sierra takes a backseat to no other area. The Sierra Nevada fault has created an enormous escarpment on the east side of the range, with possible descents of 7,000 feet or more. The combination of massive amounts of snow, high altitude, and low latitude makes for skiable conditions almost all year long.

One thing most of these peaks have in common is long descents; however, when skiing out into the sagebrush at the base of these giants, you won't find uniformly great conditions from top to bottom. Nevertheless, you can shred powder near the top, carve choice windboard on an exposed ridge, throw in a couple of turns of breakable crust, and enjoy thousands of feet of velvety corn down into the sagebrush below.

The ratings listed for these descents are dependent on the condition. It's always best to climb your route so that you know exactly what you are up against.

These peaks define the essence of "earn your turn" fun. Climbing and skiing them is a big day in anyone's book, so make sure you get an early start. If you leave too late, you may not make the summit, but you'll still have a great time. Although there may be only a few days when the conditions are perfect, these peaks are always worth the effort. Bagging one of these descents would be a skier's dream, doing them all is a lifetime goal. Keep your eyes open, too, because some of the best descents haven't been listed in this book. I encourage you to poke around, pore over maps, and peer into gullies. You never know when you might find the ultimate Sierra descent. Have fun looking!

Making turns on Pointless Peak.

1. Mount Langley (14,042')

Route:	Northeast couloir
Trailhead:	Tuttle Creek
Vertical:	About 6,500' (2,000' in couloir)
Length:	All day (or multiday)
Difficulty:	Class 4
USGS 7.5' Maps:	Mount Langley

Overview: Mount Langley is the most southerly of the Sierra's 14,000-foot peaks. The first ascent of the peak occurred by mistake. Clarence King was attempting to climb nearby Mount Whitney but was off by a few miles. Mount Langley is also one of the easiest of the Sierra's big peaks—at least in the summer—because there is a high trailhead and a good trail that goes nearly to the summit. In the winter, however, you have to start from the valley floor, and it's a whole different ball game.

The gully leading from the summit is clearly visible from Lone Pine and splits the rugged northeast side of the peak. The trip up and down the upper reaches of the drainage of Tuttle Creek takes you past some very impressive granite walls, including the south wall of Lone Pine Peak. The combination of a big vertical, a big summit, and a spectacular run makes this a worthwhile

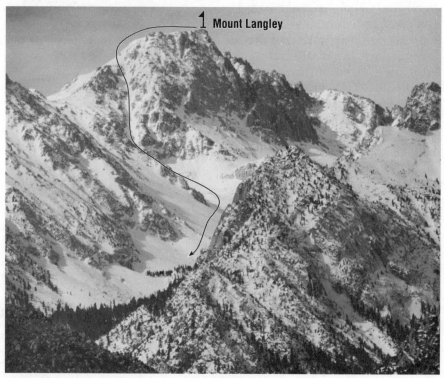

1 Mount Langley

Northeast face of Mount Langley.

adventure. Be aware that this is a big peak in a relatively remote area. Tuttle Creek Canyon doesn't get much traffic, and you should not take this trip lightly.

Route: To get to the trailhead, turn west onto Whitney Portal Road from US Highway 395 in the center of Lone Pine. After passing through the Alabama Hills, turn south on Horseshoe Meadows Road, drive a short distance, and turn west onto Tuttle Creek Campground Road. At the campground, cross the creek and follow a dirt road west as far as you can. Park near the creek at the base of the canyon (7,500').

You can also reach Tuttle Creek by turning south onto an unmarked dirt road about a mile east of the Lone Pine Campground off Whitney Portal Road. Take the left fork of the canyon as it climbs steeply up towards Mount Langley. Near the head of the canyon, you will see a prominent gully on the left leading up to the summit ridge of the peak. This chute is pretty steep, dropping about 2,000 feet. Be attentive on your way down, because there aren't many alternatives.

2   Mount Whitney (14,495')

Route:	Mountaineer's Route
Trailhead:	Whitney Portal
Vertical:	About 6,500' (2,000' in couloir)
Length:	All day (or multiday)
Difficulty:	Class 4
USGS 7.5' Maps:	Mount Whitney

Overview: This route offers the best chance to ski off the highest peak in the lower forty-eight. Don't miss it! Actually, you don't get to ski off the true summit (unless you have a death wish), but it's close enough to count. The gully looks vertical from below, but it is really not that steep. The scary part is the icy ledges leading from the top of the gully to the summit plateau. Be careful. Many people have suffered fatal falls here.

The route has plenty of history. John Muir made the first ascent of the couloir in 1873. Ever since, a descent has been the goal of many Sierra ski mountaineers. The couloir is quite obvious from Lone Pine, but getting to the route can be a little tricky. This is an example of how snow makes the routefinding easier, because here it packs down the dreaded willows in the north fork of Lone Pine Creek.

East face and Mountaineer's Route, Mount Whitney.

113

Route: To get to the trailhead, turn west onto Whitney Portal Road from US Highway 395 in the center of the town of Lone Pine. The road passes through the Alabama Hills and begins to climb the eastern escarpment of the Sierra. After a couple of switchbacks, the road ends below the impressive granite buttresses of Whitney Portal. From the parking area, follow the north fork of Lone Pine Creek. As it narrows below some cliffs, either continue up the drainage or follow the summer route up ledges on the north side of the narrow canyon to get to the upper reaches of the creek. Pass Lower Boy Scout Lake, then head south and follow the drainage up to Iceberg Lake near the base of the couloir.

Mountaineer's Route, Mount Whitney.

The ascent route is the gully, which is steep enough to require an ice axe and maybe crampons. Because the couloir faces east, it's best to get onto it early before it softens too much.

The couloir tops out a few hundred feet below and to the north of the summit. Be aware that the blocky ledges above the top of the gully face north and are usually very icy and exposed. If you want to reach the summit, you may want to bring a rope, especially for the descent back to the top of the gully. Mark the point where you gain the summit ridge, because it is not as obvious when you come back from the summit. The descent from the top of the gully is obvious, though. Return the way you came.

Skiing Mountaineer's Route.

3 Mount Williamson (14,375')

Route: North fork of Bairs Creek
Trailhead: Foothill Road
Vertical: About 8,000'
Length: All day (or multiday)
Difficulty: Class 4
USGS 7.5' Maps: Mount Williamson, Manzanar

Overview: Mount Williamson may be the second tallest peak in the Sierra, but it is by far the biggest. No one in his or her right mind would climb this route in the summer, because the brush and talus at the bottom are nearly impenetrable. In fact, this route should only be considered in heavy snow years when snow reaches the base. During a normal year, you'd have to be a little masochistic to enjoy the suffering.

Speaking of suffering, if you really are into self-abuse, the extremely steep couloirs on the north face of the peak may be just what you want. David Braun skied most of these in the spring of 1998, including the dramatic Giant Steps Couloir. As is often the case, the crux of these challenging gullies is getting to the base and then figuring out which one is which. From the trailhead at Shepherd Pass, follow Shepherd Creek to its confluence with Williamson Creek, then follow this creek to the base of the wall. It would be a good idea to take a photo with you for reference.

Bair's Creek, Mount Williamson.

North face of Mount Williamson.

Route: From US Highway 395 in the center of the town of Independence, take Onion Valley Road west until you reach Foothill Road. This rough dirt road leads south past the turnoff to the trailhead at Shepherd Pass, crosses Shepherd Creek, and climbs almost to the base of the mountain at the north fork of Bairs Creek (6,400'). To reach the enticing ski slopes above, you first must pass through the tangled brush of the steep lower canyon. Depending on the snow cover, the question is "Do I carry my skis in my hands or do I strap them on my pack?" Either method is bound to bring grief. At about 9,000 feet, the canyon finally becomes a ski route as you head up into the monstrous cirque perched on the side of the peak.

You can pass the massive headwall at the top of the right-hand cirque (12,550') but if you intend to ski the central couloir, you should ascend by that route. At the top of the headwall (13,200'), broad slopes lead to the summit plateau and the top of California's second highest peak (14,375'). Descend the way you came. If the headwall is too steep, you can ski down the moderate slopes of the south fork of Bairs Creek. As a moderate alternative, you can ski the drainage of George Creek to the south. As an extreme alternative, the steep gullies on the north face are definitely worth checking out.

4 Mount Tyndall (14,018')

> **Route:** North face
> **Trailhead:** Foothill Road
> **Vertical:** About 7,500'
> **Length:** All day (or multiday)
> **Difficulty:** Class 4
> **USGS 7.5' Maps:** Mount Williamson, Manzanar

Overview: Mount Tyndall is perhaps the most neglected of the Sierra's 14,000-foot peaks. Although visible for a moment from US Highway 395, the peak doesn't attract much attention. Even from the base of the north face near Shepherd Pass, the peak is rather inconspicuous, especially compared to its lofty neighbor Mount Williamson. Like Mount Whitney, the first ascent of the peak was made by accident. Once again, Clarence King was trying to climb Whitney and missed it by ten miles or so. Tyndall's north slopes make up for the lack of dramatic aesthetics by providing 2,000 feet of excellent skiing at a moderately steep angle. In addition, you can combine this descent with The Superbowl, which leads from a peaklet on the Sierra Crest just east of Shepherd Pass down to Mahogany Flat. This run provides 5,000 feet of great skiing and is worth the price of admission alone.

Route: To get to the Shepherd Pass trailhead, follow Onion Valley Road west from Independence until you reach Foothill Road. This dirt road leads south to the turnoff to the Shepherd Pass trailhead. Turn here and follow

North face of Mount Tyndall with Great Western Divide in background.

this rough road up to the trailhead (6,400'). From the parking area, take the trail up into the Symmes Creek drainage, climbing south over a low ridge (9,100') before traversing into the Shepherd Creek drainage at Mahogany Flat. Continue up the trail past Anvil Camp (10,000') and The Pothole (10,800') before making the final steep climb to Shepherd Pass (12,000').

From the pass, the north slopes of Mount Tyndall are directly to the south. Stay to the right (west) of the prominent north rib to reduce your exposure on the climb. At the top of the ridge, scramble out the narrow knife-edge to the actual summit (14,000'). On the descent, be sure to keep to the left of the north rib. Contour around the bowl at the base of the slope and then climb to the top of the small peaklet (13,000') east of Shepherd Pass to reach The Superbowl. Be prepared for the ride of your life. This perfectly pitched run just keeps going and going and going all the way down to the creek at Mahogany Flats. Don't succumb to the temptation to keep going beyond the flats, however, as the lower reaches of Shepherd Creek are pretty inhospitable. From the flats, take the trail over the hump into the Symmes Creek drainage and back to the car.

5 Independence Peak (11,744')

Route:	East gully
Trailhead:	Onion Valley Road
Vertical:	About 2,700'
Length:	A few hours
Difficulty:	Class 3
USGS 7.5' Maps:	Kearsarge Peak

Overview: Independence Peak was one of Norman Clyde's favorite peaks. He made over 30 ascents of the peak and must have toted his skis up this gully more than once. This moderate descent follows a very prominent avalanche path, so be careful following a storm or rapid warming trend. The roadside nature of the trip (along with the reasonable angle of the gully) makes this a fun and minimally committing adventure. It's perfect for a morning run before heading off somewhere else. If you prefer runs that are "steeper than the back of your head," check out the north couloir on the peak. This fall line horror drops straight from the summit towards Onion Valley and involves jumping a couple of cliff bands along the way. The Sierra Chute Corps chronicled their experiences in an early edition of the *Chronicle du Couloir Magazine*.

Route: This adventure starts on the road just below Onion Valley (9,000'). To get there, turn west from US Highway 395 onto Onion Valley Road in downtown Independence. The road climbs steeply up switchbacks, passing Sardine Canyon Road (closed) before turning west again toward Onion Valley.

East side of Independence Peak.

Park off the road in a place not threatened by rockfall and drop down to the creek. Cross the creek and ascend on a gradually steeper slope into the gully proper. The gully corkscrews its way towards the summit, first heading south, then west, and finally north to reach the last steep section to the rocky summit (11,744'). You can turn around at any point, especially if the corn bomb is going off, and return to the car. If your goal is the more radical north couloir, climb that route directly from the road.

6   University Peak (13,632')

Route:	North face
Trailhead:	Onion Valley
Vertical:	4,400'
Length:	Half day
Difficulty:	Class 3
USGS 7.5' Maps:	Kearsarge Peak, Mount Clarence King

Oveview: There is plenty of history associated with University Peak and the general area. Miners explored the area during the Civil War and sympathizers on both sides named many of the local features, such as the Alabama Hills and Kearsarge Peak—both names commemorating warships. Joseph LeConte named University Peak after his *alma mater* University of California-Berkeley in response to his rival Bolton Brown's naming of nearby Mount Stanford.

Northeast face of University Peak.

Old-timers used to consider the Kearsarge area one of the finest spring locations in the eastern Sierra. Every year skiers would set up a rope tow at Onion Valley and tear up the surrounding slopes. Now, the rope tow is long gone and the attention has turned to the higher peaks. Norman Clyde made the first ascent of this route, but the records don't show if he ever skied it. I like to think that he did. Norman loved to ski, and this run would have held his fancy. University Peak is the tallest and most attractive peak along this section of the crest, and the view from the summit is excellent. There are a number of fine runs off the summit, but the best one is down the north face.

Route: This classic adventure starts at Onion Valley. To get there, turn west off US Highway 395 onto Onion Valley Road in downtown Independence. Depending on the time of year, the road may be clear all the way to Onion Valley, although normally you will have to park a few switchbacks down. From Onion Valley (9,200'), follow the course of Independence Creek as it stairsteps up past Little Pothole Lake (10,050') and Gilbert Lake (10,475') to Flower Lake (10,525'). Along the way, there are spectacular views of the peak. From the lake, head southwest over a low ridge to the Matlock Lakes and the base of the north face. Then climb the route to the narrow summit ridge. A bit of scrambling takes you to the summit. Enjoy the fine run down the north face back to the car.

7 Kearsarge Peak (12,598')

Route: Sardine Canyon
Trailhead: Onion Valley
Vertical: About 5,000'
Length: Half day
Difficulty: Class 3
USGS 7.5' Maps: Kearsarge Peak

Overview: Sardine Canyon is one of the coolest ski descents in the eastern Sierra. The broad gullies descending the northeast slopes of Kearsarge Peak are really fun—steep enough to be interesting, but not too scary. This run is surprisingly long, even though the summit is lower than 13,000 feet. Along the way, you pass the ruins of an old mining operation, adding some local color and historical interest. The old mining road skirting the east side of the peak provides a convenient return route to Onion Valley Road following the descent. As a bonus, you may get to see some bighorn sheep from the Baxter Pass herd. Please do not disturb these magnificent animals if you can help it.

Route: This adventure also starts at Onion Valley (9,200'). To get there, turn west off US Highway 395 onto Onion Valley Road in downtown Independence. The road climbs steeply up switchbacks, passing Sardine Canyon Road (closed) before turning west again toward Onion Valley. Early in the season the road may not be cleared all the way to the end. If so, park off the

Sardine Canyon, Kearsarge Peak.

road in a place not threatened by rockfall. From the trailhead, begin by climbing alongside the outlet stream of the Golden Trout Lakes. At the junction of the two forks of the drainage (11,000'), follow a steep gully northeast, then scramble north onto the summit ridge and the top of Kearsarge Peak (12,598'). The open gullies below your feet drop steeply into Sardine Canyon. Once you reach the bottom of the canyon, continue down the drainage until you get to a mining road (7,200'), which takes you back around the east slopes of the peak to Onion Valley Road. By arranging a shuttle, it is possible to get an extra 2,000-foot descent below the original starting point. The disadvantage is that by ascending a different route, you won't know what conditions will be like for the descent.

8 Mount Perkins-East Peak (11,765')

Route:	Spook Canyon
Trailhead:	Sawmill Creek
Vertical:	About 5,500'
Length:	A few hours
Difficulty:	Class 4
USGS 7.5" Maps:	Aberdeen

Overview: Spook Canyon and Pinnacle Gully (to the north) provide two of the most striking ski lines in the eastern Sierra. Plainly visible from US Highway 395 in the vicinity of Blackrock Springs and Aberdeen, these impressive gullies lie to the east of the crest on the east peak of Mount Perkins. Spook Canyon is a plumb line, dropping due east from the summit. It is very steep and melts out early down low, so you need to time your descent. The next canyon north offers a slightly less extreme descent, but it is still plenty challenging. This route passes a number of mines, including the Pinnacle Mine, thus the name, Pinnacle Gully. If these runs are too steep, neighboring Armstrong Canyon provides a very long and moderate descent.

Route: To reach these runs, take Division Creek Road from US Highway 395 past the powerhouse; then follow the pipeline road as it ascends past the trailhead for Sawmill Pass to Scotty Springs (6,000'). To reach the east peak of Mount Perkins (11,765'), which is directly above Scotty Springs, follow the shallow gully to the north. Take the old mining road past the gate, and switchback onto the ridge to the north. The ascent gully usually offers the best descent, while Spook Canyon provides an extremely steep and narrow drop straight down to the car. Armstrong Canyon is the moderate valley heading towards the crest from the Rudy Mine (8,400'). It is possible to ascend this canyon all the way to the Sierra Crest. A steep headwall reaches the crest just south of the summit of Mount Perkins (12,591'). The fine run

Spook Canyon, Mount Perkins.

down the canyon brings you into the high desert and is followed by a long traverse back around to the car.

9 Split Mountain (14,058')

Route: Northeast couloir
Trailhead: McMurray Meadows
Vertical: About 6,000'
Length: All day (or multiday)
Difficulty: Class 5
USGS 7.5' Maps: Split Mountain, Fish Springs

Overview: Split Mountain was once known as South Palisade, and it certainly deserves to be included with the fine Palisades peaks. The central couloir, which splits two of the most impressive arêtes on the northeast face, is considered one of the classic (and most difficult) ice climbs in the range. The crux is a nearly vertical ice headwall near the bottom of the couloir. Above this, the gully provides a long, moderately steep run. A number of prominent Sierra mountaineers have been involved with this couloir. Bob Harrington made the first ascent, climbing solo around the ice crux. Yvon Chouinard, Richard Leversee, and James Wilson were the first to tackle

Northeast face of Split Mountain.

the headwall crux of the gully. Famed extreme skier Glen Plake is credited with the first ski descent of the gully, including a rappel over the crux. Leversee later returned with Jim Zellers for the first snowboard descent. Surprisingly enough, the gully above the crux is not that serious, but getting over the headwall at the base (in either direction) certainly is.

Route: This is another peak where getting to the base is the real crux. The most straightforward route (from Fish Springs/Tinemaha Creek) passes through private property and is not recommended. A longer, but more certain, approach involves getting to McMurray Meadows. At the traffic light in Big Pine, turn west on Glacier Lodge Road and drive through the residential neighborhood. On the outskirts of town, pass the Bernasconi Learning Center and turn left onto the road to McMurray Meadows. Follow this long and bumpy road as it winds its way up to McMurray Meadows (6,500'). If possible, continue on the road to Red Mountain Creek; then follow the steep trail to Red Lake (10,500').

Continue west up increasingly steep slopes to reach the base of the couloir (12,000'). The gully is blocked from view until you are just below it. Attack the headwall and gain the gully above. You may want to rig a rappel anchor here. Eventually you reach the notch between the twin summits. The north summit (14,058') is slightly higher. If the gully looks too steep or icy, you can always opt for the St. Jean or Clyde couloirs (Class 4) just to the north, which access the north ridge of the peak. Either way, you'll be guaranteed an exciting and aesthetic trip down one of the range's most impressive peaks.

10 Birch Mountain (13,685')

Route: Southeast slopes
Trailhead: McMurray Meadows
Vertical: About 6,000'
Length: All day
Difficulty: Class 3
USGS 7.5' Maps: Split Mountain, Fish Springs

Overview: The southeast slopes of Birch Mountain offer another of the classic, big eastside descents. The best place to view the route is from US Highway 395 south of Big Pine near the lava flows of Crater Mountain. Like Mount Williamson, Birch Mountain is a massive, solitary peak whose summit looms about 10,000 feet directly above Owens Valley. Even so, the peak is pretty remote and demands respect. Because the run faces southeast, this descent is only recommended in big snow years when the snow extends well down towards the valley floor. In big snow years, this route can offer up to 6,000 feet of perfect spring corn at a very consistent and moderate angle. And, because of the orientation, the southeast slope of Birch Mountain comes into condition earlier in the year than most of the other descents listed in this book.

Route: Like for Mount Williamson, finding the route to the base of this giant can sometimes be the crux. At the traffic light in Big Pine, turn west on Glacier Lodge Road and drive through the residential neighborhood. On

Southeast side of Birch Mountain.

Backcountry boarding in Bishop Creek.

the outskirts of town, pass the Bernasconi Learning Center and then turn left onto the road to McMurray Meadows just after crossing Big Pine Creek for the first time. Follow this long and bumpy road as it winds its way up to the hidden paradise of McMurray Meadows (6,500'). At the south end of the meadows, a faint trail leads up into the Tinemaha Creek drainage. Follow the brushy drainage west toward the huge cirque below Mount Bolton Brown, then climb the southeast slopes of Birch Mountain to the summit (13,685'). There is a great view of The Palisades from here. Retrace the route for the descent.

11 Kid Mountain (11,896')

Route: North slopes
Trailhead: Glacier Lodge
Vertical: About 4,200'
Length: A few hours
Difficulty: Class 3
USGS 7.5' Maps: Split Mountain

Overview: Kid Mountain is certainly a big kid's playground with a wide variety of chutes to tempt a backcountry skier. These chutes are frequent avalanche performers, so take care in evaluating the potential hazard. H.J.

North and east sides of Kid Mountain.

Burhenne profiled this peak in his 1971 book stating, "It may look like a kid's mountain, but it is not. The length of the hill and the climb are full size." The view of the neighboring Palisades from the top is very impressive and worth the climb. However, the run down any of these natural half-pipes is the main attraction. To get a sense of snow conditions, your best bet is to climb the route of your chosen descent.

Route: At the traffic light on US Highway 395 in downtown Big Pine, turn west onto Glacier Lodge Road and climb steeply up the course of Big Pine Creek. After a few switchbacks, you get a view of the big hulk of Birch Mountain, with the smaller (but still impressive) Kid Mountain just to the north. Continue up the road to the trailhead parking area. From here, you have a choice of at least one-half dozen major gullies. The one just east of Glacier Lodge is as good as any. Cross the creek at the lodge (7,700') and head up the avalanche cone to get to the lower reaches of the gully, then follow the gully forever to reach the summit (11,896'). Your car will be directly below your tips as you take in the view and drop in for the fun ride down.

12   Mount Sill (14,162')

Route:	North couloir
Trailhead:	Glacier Lodge
Vertical:	About 6,300'
Length:	Multiday
Difficulty:	Class 4
USGS 7.5' Maps:	Split Mountain, North Palisade, Coyote Flat, Mount Thompson

Overview: Mount Sill, one of the giants of the Sierra, is a prominent landmark from many points in the region. The native people called it the "Watcher of the Valley," and the view from the summit is considered one of the best in the range. The east side of the peak is a very impressive cliff, while the north side is only slightly more broken. Neither side offers much in the way of a ski descent; however, two prominent gullies drape the northeast corner of the peak, beginning at the saddle (Apex Col) between the main summit and a subsidiary summit known as Apex Peak. The gully leading east, which is called the L-Shaped Couloir for its distinctive geometry, leads down to the saddle of Glacier Notch. The north couloir drops steeply from Apex Col to the Palisade Glacier below. This gully was made famous in a number of North Face catalogs in the mid-1980s with photographs of Chris Cox dropping in as part of the Redline Traverse.

Route: To reach the Palisade Glacier, drive west off US Highway 395 from the center of Big Pine on Glacier Lodge Road. Just before the lodge, there is an overnight parking area. From Glacier Lodge (7,800'), follow the trail along

North couloir on Mount Sill.

the North Fork of Big Pine Creek past First Falls and into the shallow basin below Second Falls (8,500'). Enjoy the view of the dark towers of Temple Crag as you make the gentle climb through sparse timber, following the creek up to First Lake (10,000'). You pass high above Second Lake before arriving at the stunning location of Third Lake (10,250') at the foot of Temple Crag.

From the lake, don't follow the summer trail, but rather climb the steep gully to the west below the imposing north faces of Temple Crag and Mount Gayley to reach the terminal moraine of the Palisade Glacier (12,150'). From the glacier, skirt the north side of Mount Sill to reach the base of the north couloir. Cross the bergschrund (note the position of the lip for the descent) and climb the couloir to the col (13,800'). If you want to bag the peak, make an exposed and icy traverse west across ledges to reach the west ridge of Mount Sill. The summit (14,162') is a short scramble to the east. Carefully descend back to the col and rip it up.

13   North Palisade (14,242')

Route: U-Notch Couloir
Trailhead: Glacier Lodge
Vertical: About 6,300'
Length: Multiday
Difficulty: Class 4-5
USGS 7.5' Maps: Split Mountain, North Palisade, Coyote Flat, Mount Thompson

Overview: The U-Notch Couloir has long been considered one of the premier extreme descents, as well as one of the classic ice climbs, in the Sierra. The trick is to catch it when the snow is good and the gaping bergschrund is passable. There are three cruxes. First, the top is very steep and intimidating. Second, the gully has a double fall line with an annoying habit of drawing toward the rocks on the side. Finally, the bergschrund can be a major mind trip, not to mention big air, as you leap to avoid the icy depths below. Getting to the summit of the peak is a different story, however, and involves some moderate rock climbing out of the gully or some serious routefinding on the southwest side of the peak. I suggest sticking to the sliding stuff. If this gully isn't sick enough, there's always the neighboring V-Notch and Clyde couloirs. All of the North Palisade gullies finish with big air over their gaping bergschrunds. Be afraid. Be very afraid.

Route: To reach the Palisade Glacier area, drive west off US Highway 395 from the center of Big Pine on Glacier Lodge Road. Just before the lodge, there is an overnight parking area. From Glacier Lodge (7,800'), follow the trail along the North Fork of Big Pine Creek past First Falls and into the shallow basin below Second Falls (8,500'). Enjoy the view of the dark towers of Temple Crag as you make the gentle climb through sparse timber, following the creek up to First Lake (10,000'). You'll pass high above Second Lake before arriving at the stunning location of Third Lake (10,250') at the foot of Temple Crag.

From the lake, don't follow the summer trail, but rather climb the steep gully to the west below the imposing north faces of Temple Crag, Mount Gayley, and Mount Sill to reach the terminal moraine of the Palisade Glacier (12,150'). Continue up the glacier to the left of the peak and head for the obvious couloir below the well-named notch. Cross the bergschrund where possible (this is often easiest on climber's right) and climb the couloir to the notch (14,000'). If this run isn't thrilling enough, The V-Notch just to

Palisade Glacier, Mount Sill to Thunderbolt Peak.

U-Notch and V-Notch on North Palisades.

the east is even steeper and narrower. It tops out on a subsidiary summit known as Polemonium Peak. Clyde Couloir on the face of North Palisade has also been skied (by local Jon-Marc Baker) but is not recommended due the narrow confines and frequent rockfall.

14 Thunderbolt Peak (14,000')

Route:	North face
Trailhead:	Glacier Lodge
Vertical:	About 6,100'
Length:	Multiday
Difficulty:	Class 4
USGS 7.5' Maps:	Split Mountain, North Palisade, Coyote Flat, Mount Thompson

Overview: The Palisade Glacier area is perhaps the single finest place in the range to hang out and ski steep gullies. The region has long been considered the most alpine section of the Sierra and is home to a high concentration of fine mountaineering routes. The same goes for sliding. Thunderbolt Peak was the last 14,000-foot peak in the Sierra to be climbed, and the name reflects an unfortunate encounter with lightning on the first ascent. On the east shoulder of the peak, there is a series of short, steep couloirs named for Robert Underhill, leader of the first ascent team. The Underhill Couloirs

North Glacier on Thunderbolt Peak.

offer an exciting diversion, but the real attraction is the north face. This broad face is not really a couloir but more like a smaller version of the ice shields found in the Alps or Canadian Rockies. The actual summit is a tall monolith that is quite difficult. The trick is to throw a rope over it, anchor it well, and Batman up.

Route: To reach the Palisade Glacier area, drive west off US Highway 395 from the center of Big Pine on Glacier Lodge Road. Just before the lodge, there is an overnight parking area. From Glacier Lodge (7,800'), follow the trail along the North Fork of Big Pine Creek past First Falls and into the shallow basin below Second Falls (8,500'). Enjoy the view of the dark towers of Temple Crag as you make the gentle climb through sparse timber following the creek up to First Lake (10,000'). You'll pass high above Second Lake before arriving at the stunning location of Third Lake (10,250') at the foot of Temple Crag.

From the lake, don't follow the summer trail, but rather climb the steep gully to the west below the imposing north faces of Temple Crag, Mount Gayley, and Mount Sill to reach the terminal moraine of the Palisade Glacier (12,150'). Follow the moraine towards the prominent prow that leads northeast from the summit of Thunderbolt Peak. The Underhill Couloirs are on the left side of the prow and the north slope is on the right. Gain the base of the slope, cross the bergschrund, and then continue up to the east summit (14,000'). The long run down is plenty steep, although not quite in the realm of some of the more famous couloirs in the neighborhood.

15 Hurd Peak (12,219')

Route:	North couloir
Trailhead:	South Lake
Vertical:	About 2,500'
Length:	A few hours
Difficulty:	Class 4-5
USGS 7.5' Maps:	Mount Thompson

Overview: This peak may be short on altitude, but it makes up for it in attitude. The north couloir is right in front of your face at the parking area at South Lake. From the dam, this steep gully looks dead vertical, but in reality it's only near-vertical. The first 1,000 feet average well over 40 degrees, so you definitely want to be confident of your edges here. Hurd Peak also harbors a nasty sting in the tail because the bottom cliff is the steepest part of the route. This descent is definitely not for everyone, but if you've got it, flaunt it. Have your video crew film your descent from the dam and get ready for extreme sports stardom.

Route: From US Highway 395 in downtown Bishop, turn west onto California 168 (West Line Street), and climb through the desert into Bishop Creek Canyon. Turn left (south) onto South Lake Road and continue to the end of the road. Depending on the snowpack, this may be at Bishop Creek Lodge, Parchers Lodge, or the dam at South Lake. From the dam (9,755'), take the

North face of Hurd Peak.

summer trail until you can follow Bishop Creek up to the outlet of Long Lake (10,750'). Contour around to the west until you are below the main couloir on the north side of Hurd Peak. Climb the gully to test the snow conditions before committing to the descent. Near the top, the angle eases off, but the summit ridge is a knife-edge blocking access to the summit (12,200'). If you're still up for the run, more power to you.

16 Mount Gilbert (13,103')

Route:	East couloir
Trailhead:	South Lake
Vertical:	About 3,300'
Length:	Half day
Difficulty:	Class 4
USGS 7.5' Maps:	Mount Thompson

Overview: As with neighboring Mount Thompson, Mount Gilbert offers a couple of interesting ski descents. The northwest couloir has long been considered one of the classic ice climbs in the range and offers a very steep run from the notch to the northwest of the peak. Because this shot does not provide easy access to the summit, the scale tips towards the east couloir as the best descent. In addition, this east couloir allows access to the enjoyable bowls above the Treasure Lakes. You can see this steep shot, which reaches

North glacier on Mount Gilbert.

Stephen Pope skiing Mount Gilbert's north couloir.

the col to the left of the peak, from the dam at South Lake. At this point, it is possible to ski from the main summit or the subsidiary peak to the east. In either case, this run is one of the best in the range and provides an excellent introduction to steep couloir skiing in the Sierra backcountry, without being too far from the road.

Route: From US Highway 395 in downtown Bishop, turn west onto California 168 (West Line Street) and climb through the desert into Bishop Creek Canyon. Turn left (south) onto South Lake Road and continue to the end of the road. Depending on the snowpack, this may be at Bishop Creek Lodge, Parchers Lodge, or the dam at South Lake. From the dam (9,755'), skirt the edge of the lake until you reach the inlet creek on the south side, which drains the Treasure Lakes. Follow the course of the creek up to the biggest lake (10,650'), then head up to the right of a prominent triangular peak into the cirque on the east side of Mount Gilbert (12,000'). The gully is dead center and very steep. The top of the couloir may be blocked by a cornice. Once at the col, continue up and left to the peak between Mount Johnson and Mount Gilbert, or head west to the summit of Mount Gilbert (13,100'). Why not bag both and double your fun?

17 Mount Thompson (13,440')

Route:	Northeast couloirs
Trailhead:	South Lake
Vertical:	About 3,700'
Length:	Half day
Difficulty:	Class 4
USGS 7.5' Maps:	Mount Thompson

Overview: The area around Mount Thompson offers a wide variety of ski descents. The Alpine Expeditions used to maintain a base camp, which was wiped out by an avalanche in 1986. The subsidiary peak to the north of Mount Thompson has been referred to as Ski Mountaineers Peak and offers an enjoyable run down its east side. While neighboring Mount Gilbert harbors a very steep gully on its northwest flanks that ranks as one of the classic ice climbs in the range, it is the cluster of steep gullies on the northeast side of Mount Thompson that is the real attraction. At the far eastern edge of the peak, there is a trio of gullies that look like Neptune's trident. Each offers about 1,000 feet of steep skiing at a consistent pitch. Norman Clyde made the first ascent of these gullies in the 1930s using hobnailed boots and a long ice axe. There is also a very steep gully splitting the middle of the north wall of the peak. This narrow shot, which is similar to the Mendel Couloir, should be considered only by the boldest extreme skiers.

Mount Gilbert and Thompson Cirque on Mount Thompson.

Route: From US Highway 395 in downtown Bishop, turn west onto California 168 (West Line Street) and climb through the desert into Bishop Creek Canyon. Turn left (south) onto South Lake Road and continue to the end of the road. Depending on the snowpack, this may be at Bishop Creek Lodge, Parchers Lodge, or the dam at South Lake. From the dam (9,755'), skirt the edge of the lake until you reach the inlet creek on the south side, which drains the Treasure Lakes. Follow the course of the creek up toward the lakes; then climb up the low ridge to the west to reach a series of small lakes (11,600') at the bottom of the cirque below Mount Gilbert and Mount Thompson. Head west toward the saddle between Ski Mountaineers Peak and Mount Thompson until you can see the gullies. Climb your chosen pitch to the summit plateau (13,200'). The summit (13,440') is about one-half mile to the west. Unfortunately, there is no easy way down. If the gullies are too intimidating to ski, you'll have to climb back down them or use the north ridge (Class 3) as an escape route.

18 Table Mountain (10,584')

Route: Bardini Canyon
Trailhead: Four Jeffreys Campground
Vertical: About 2,300'
Length: A few hours
Difficulty: Class 3
USGS 7.5' Maps: Mount Thompson

Overview: While this descent is not as huge as many in the neighborhood, it is an afternoon delight, requiring little time or commitment. There is a great variety of gullies to choose from on the north end of Table Mountain, ranging from the natural half pipes near Bishop Creek Lodge to the steep face runs above Aspendel. The best run leads due north from the northernmost point and follows a shallow gully back down to Four Jeffreys Campground. This is a local favorite and has become known as Bardini Canyon in memory of Allan Bard, who used to ski this run frequently from his home in Bishop. This descent is best as a winter powder run, but it can also provide good skiing in the spring.

Route: From US Highway 395 in downtown Bishop, turn west onto California 168 (West Line Street) and climb up through the desert into Bishop Creek Canyon. Turn left (south) onto South Lake Road and park at the turnout for Four Jeffreys Campground (8,200'). Bardini Canyon begins in the shallow gully just south of the right-hand skyline. Follow this to the top of the northernmost knoll of Table Mountain (10,584'); then turn around, pay your respects to Bardini, and whoop it up on the way down.

Bardini Canyon, Table Mountain.

John Dostal skiing Bardini Canyon on Table Mountain.

19 Mount Darwin (13,830')

Route: North face
Trailhead: North Lake
Vertical: About 5,500' (total)
Length: Multiday
Difficulty: Class 4
USGS 7.5' Maps: Mount Darwin

Overview: Massive Mount Darwin dominates the Evolution region, and the north face of the peak holds one of the few ice/snow shields in the Sierra, making it an attractive ski objective. The actual summit of the peak is a small detached pinnacle on the eastern edge of the summit plateau. The crux of the descent is the narrow couloir dropping from the summit plateau onto the broad glacier below. The entry to this couloir is often blocked by a cornice and the angle is over 45 degrees for several hundred feet. In 1980, noted extreme skier Chris Landry used this route as a warm-up for skiing neighboring Mendel Couloir. This protocol was repeated by Andrew McLean in 1998 when he made the second descent (first complete) of the Mendel. Tom Carter and the crew from Alpine Expeditions made the first Nordic descent of the route as part of the Redline Traverse.

Route: To reach the trailhead at North Lake, turn west off US Highway 395 onto California 168 (West Line Street) in the center of the town of Bishop

North face of Mount Darwin. VERN CLEVENGER PHOTO

and continue west for 14 miles toward Lake Sabrina to the turnoff to North Lake. Early in the season, you will have to park here. Otherwise, follow the steep dirt road up to the parking area on the west side of the lake (9,400'). From the lake, take the steep trail to Upper Lamarck Lake, then climb the steep slope to the southwest to gain the hanging valley that leads to Lamarck Col (13,000'). At the pass, both Mount Darwin and Mount Mendel are painfully obvious. Descend the west side of the pass until you are able to contour around to the base of the peak. From the moraine (12,400'), climb the glacier (watch for the small bergschrund) and enter the prominent central couloir. Near the top, the gully cuts to the left before reaching the summit plateau (13,830'). If conditions are icy or a cornice blocks your path, you may want to begin your descent from the rock buttress on skier's left of the couloir.

20 Mount Mendel (13,691')

Route:	Right Mendel Couloir
Trailhead:	North Lake
Vertical:	About 5,200' (total)
Length:	Multiday
Difficulty:	Class 5
USGS 7.5' Maps:	Mount Darwin

Overview: The Mendel Couloir has been considered THE extreme ski descent in the Sierra ever since Chris Landry pasted turns on the seemingly vertical confines of the couloir in 1980. The second recorded descent was not until 1998, when Andrew McLean and Mark Holbrook answered the challenge. McLean noted that "The Mendel obeys all the unwritten rules of a classic ski descent... in legal terms it could be considered an attractive hazard." Viewed across Darwin Canyon, the gully seems dead vertical and many a bold skier has turned tail here. The central ice bulge has been measured at close to 60 degrees and is generally free of snow. Following a heavy El Niño winter, McLean found most of the gully to be powder snow over ice at an angle between 50 and 55 degrees except for this bulge. The two options for passing this dicey section are downclimbing (Landry) or side-slipping with a handline (McLean). Either way, this route is a run of a lifetime for those few skiers/boarders competent enough to link turns in such an intimidating place.

Route: To reach the trailhead at North Lake, turn west off US Highway 395 onto California 168 (West Line Street) in the center of the town of Bishop and continue west toward Lake Sabrina and the turnoff to North Lake. Early in the season, you will have to park here. Otherwise, follow the steep dirt road up to the parking area on the west side of the lake (9,400'). From the

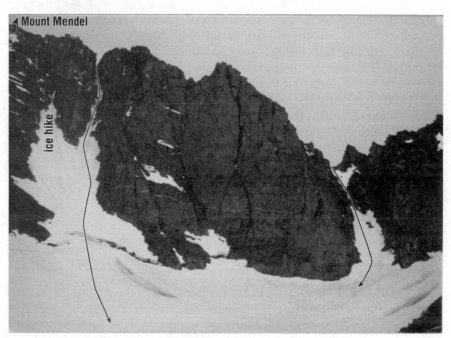

ice hike

Mount Mendel

North face of Mount Mendel.

walk-in campground west of the lake, take the steep trail to Lamarck Lakes. From the upper lake, climb the steep slope to the southwest to gain the hanging valley that leads to Lamarck Col (13,000'). Look up and there it is—many skiers have lost heart and turned around here. Descend the west side of the pass until you are able to contour around past the base of Mount Darwin to the base of Mount Mendel. Upon reaching the small glacier at the base, begin climbing the initial apron until it gets steeper at the throat. From here, climb as high as you dare before giving in to gravity. The narrow top of the gully never holds enough snow to warrant even the sickest thoughts of skiing from the summit.

21 Mount Lamarck (13,417')

Route:	North couloir
Trailhead:	North Lake
Vertical:	About 4,000'
Length:	All day
Difficulty:	Class 4
USGS 7.5' Maps:	Mount Darwin

Overview: You can see the flat-topped summit ridge of Mount Lamarck (along with its two prominent snow couloirs) from the west side of Bishop.

These gullies provide a good introduction to the more extreme descents in the area. Skiers have long considered the run from Lamarck Col a classic descent, but for modern skiers looking for more of a challenge, these gullies are just the ticket. Perhaps the best way to access this descent is by touring up the Lamarck Col route, then picking the run from the summit of the peak. This provides the easiest and most aesthetic tour, but you don't know what the snow conditions will be for the descent. If you're really worried about the conditions, then just return the way you came—the run will still be very memorable.

Route: To reach the trailhead at North Lake, turn west off US Highway 395 onto California 168 (West Line Street) in the center of the town of Bishop and continue west for 14 miles toward Lake Sabrina to the turnoff to North Lake. Early in the season, you will have to park here. Otherwise, follow the steep dirt road up to the parking area on the west side of the lake (9,400'). From the walk-in campground west of the lake, follow the steep trail leading to Lamarck Lakes. From the upper lake, climb the steep slope to the southwest to gain the hanging valley that leads to Lamarck Col (13,000'). The summit (13,417') is a short climb to the north.

The main couloir drops off the summit plateau at the obvious notch to the west of the top and takes a steep fall line to the glacier below. From the glacier, drop down the moraine to reach Upper Lamarck Lake. If this route is too steep, there is a slightly more moderate couloir to the east of the summit that also drops to the glacier. If both of these are too spicy, then return down the route you came up. From Lamarck Lakes, drop down the steep forested slope to Grass Lake, then continue down to North Lake.

Lamarch Col and Mount Lamarck.

22 Mount Emerson (13,225')

Route: North couloir
Trailhead: McGee Creek
Vertical: About 4,800'
Length: Half day
Difficulty: Class 4-5
USGS 7.5' Maps: Mount Tom

Overview: While this couloir is probably one the least known of the many great ski descents in the Buttermilk area, it has a long history—first climbed by the legendary Sierra climber Norman Clyde in 1926. No one knows who made the first descent of this aesthetic line, but it became more popular with the extreme crowd in the mid-1990s. Glen Plake, Davey McCoy, Jim and Bonnie Zellers, and others left their tracks in the colorful confines of the couloir. The gully averages well over 40 degrees for its entire length and the top is quite narrow. A short distance to the east, there is another fine gully bordered by wildly striped rock. This is known as the Zebra Couloir and was done on a board by Bonnie Zellers in 1997. There are other gullies farther to the west towards the crest, as well as around the corner to the east among the colorful Piute Crags.

Route: The peaks of the Buttermilk area are quite visible from downtown Bishop. To get there, turn off US Highway 395 onto California 168 in the center of the town of Bishop and go west about 5 miles. Turn right onto the

Mount Emerson, Mount Locke and Peak 13,112'.

dirt Buttermilk Road, drive past the Peabody Boulders, and continue up into the high desert of the Buttermilk country (7,800'). About a mile past the turn for Basin Mountain, the road reaches a cattle guard and passes through a pretty meadow with aspen trees.

There are nice campsites for a base camp at the crossing of McGee Creek (high-clearance vehicles recommended). Climb the moraine past the crossing and take the rough road on the right to another junction near a creek gauging station. The road is often impassable, even to four-wheel-drive vehicles, beyond this point. Follow the road or the creek up to the meadow (8,400') below Longley Reservoir. Mount Locke is the peak just to the southwest. Skirt the eastern slopes of Mount Locke to reach the drainage below the north face of Mount

Zebra Couloir (left) and North Couloir (right), Mount Emerson. RICHARD LEVERSEE PHOTO

Emerson. The Zebra Couloir and North Couloir should be staring you right in the face by now. Not much more needs to be said; climb the thing safely and hang on to the hill on the descent.

23 Mount Locke (12,500')

> **Route:** Wahoo Gullies
> **Trailhead:** McGee Creek
> **Vertical:** About 4,000'
> **Length:** A few hours
> **Difficulty:** Class 3-4
> **USGS 7.5' Maps:** Mount Tom

Overview: Mount Locke is not mentioned on any maps, but it has long been called Mount Locke in memory of Sierra skier and climber Bob Locke. Bob-O, as was he was known, was killed in a climbing accident on Mount Watkins in the late 1970s. In addition to fellow Yosemite climbers like Dale and Allan Bard, Chris Falkenstein, Werner Braun, and Walter Rosenthal, Bob-O made many daring first descents along the east side of the range. There are five gullies on the northeast face of the peak, rising from the avalanche cone at the base like a skeletal hand. The main Wahoo Gully is the middle finger. This gully has become one of the must-do's for visiting skiers, and, for many locals, it is the ultimate Rite of Spring, with some skiers nursing a string of more than twenty years of annual trips to pay their respects to the Great Wahoo.

Route: The peaks of the Buttermilk area are quite visible from downtown Bishop. To get there, turn onto California 168 from US Highway 395 in the center of the town of Bishop and go west about 5 miles. Turn right onto the dirt Buttermilk Road, drive past the Peabody Boulders, and continue up into the high desert of the Buttermilk country (7,800'). About a mile past the turn for Basin Mountain, the road reaches a cattle guard and passes through a pretty meadow with aspen trees.

There are nice campsites at the crossing of McGee Creek (high-

Wahoo Gully, Mount Locke. RICHARD LEVERSEE PHOTO

Jim Zellers riding the flank of Mount Locke.
RICHARD LEVERSEE PHOTO

clearance vehicles recommended). Climb the moraine past the crossing and take the rough road on the right to another junction near a creek gauging station. The road is often impassable, even to four-wheel-drive vehicles, beyond this point. Follow the road or the creek up to the meadow (8,400') below Longley Reservoir.

The white granite peak of Mount Locke (12,241') is just to the southwest of the parking area. There are five gullies on the northeast face—all of them are quite steep. The middle finger is the most attractive and popular. If conditions aren't right, the southeast slope of Mount Locke is more moderate, offering the best descent in early season or times of high avalanche hazard. If you're still looking for more challenge, check out Checkered Demon Couloir just a little bit farther up the drainage to the west.

24 Peak 13,112'

Route: Checkered Demon Couloir
Trailhead: McGee Creek
Vertical: About 4,500'
Length: Half day
Difficulty: Class 5
USGS 7.5' Maps: Mount Tom

Overview: In 1972, during the early days of modern Sierra ice climbing, Doug Robinson and John Fischer made the first ascent of this nasty looking couloir on a stormy fall day. The Checkered Demon name comes from the Tarot. More recently, a few visionary skiers and snowboarders have tried their luck. This route is essentially like skiing an elevator shaft in a building that is falling down. It is best on a cold day because of the horrendous hazard from rockfall. The peak is not made of typical Sierra granite, but rather a pendant of the old, rotten metamorphic rock.

You can just barely see this very steep couloir from US Highway 395 in the vicinity of Mill Creek to the north of Bishop. A prominent spur keeps it hidden but hints at the line behind it. Immediately to the left, there is a more moderate gully known as the Kindergarten Chute. Although this couloir is still plenty steep, it is much less committing than the neighboring Checkered Demon, thus the name. Of course, it's easy to get distracted by

Mount Locke, Peak 13,112' and Mount Humphreys.

Kindergarten Chute on Peak 13,112'. Richard Leversee photo

the attractive Wahoo Gullies on the way to the peak, especially if you're not feeling up to wrestling the Demon that day.

Route: The peaks of the Buttermilk area are quite visible from downtown Bishop. To get there, turn onto California 168 from US Highway 395 in the center of the town of Bishop and go west about 5 miles. Turn right onto the dirt Buttermilk Road, drive past the Peabody Boulders, and continue up into the high desert of the Buttermilk country (7,800'). About a mile past the turn for Basin Mountain, the road reaches a cattle guard and passes through a pretty meadow with aspen trees.

There are nice campsites at the crossing of McGee Creek (high-clearance vehicles recommended). Climb the moraine past the crossing and take the rough road on the

Checkered Demon Couloir on Peak 13,112'.
RICHARD LEVERSEE PHOTO

right to another junction near a creek gauging station. The road is often impassable, even to four-wheel-drive vehicles, beyond this point. Follow the road or the creek up to the meadow (8,400') below Longley Reservoir. Mount Locke and the Wahoo Gullies are immediately to the southwest.

Bonnie Zellers riding Checkered Demon Couloir.
RICHARD LEVERSEE PHOTO

Continue up the drainage below the gullies and ascend a short, steep rise. The rock changes from granite to shale here, so keep well away from the base of the cliffs. The Kindergarten Chute is the first gully on the left. The Demon is hidden behind a rock spur just a short way beyond. The top of the couloir is close to 50 degrees and extremely narrow. Check the Tarot before betting your life.

25 Mount Humphreys (13,986')

Route:	Northeast couloir
Trailhead:	McGee Creek
Vertical:	About 5,500'
Length:	All day
Difficulty:	Class 4-5
USGS 7.5' Maps:	Mount Tom

Overview: In the mid-1980s, there was a well-known poster of Tom Carter skiing this gully on his state-of-the-art Karhu Comps. As with most of the other gullies in the area, this run is another very steep line that becomes a classic ice climb later in the year. Humphreys Glacier is pretty large by Sierra standards and there is a good-sized bergschrund at the juncture between the couloir and glacier. Also, the top may be blocked by a cornice, making entry into this dicey gully even more hairy. The gully tops out at a small col on the north ridge of the peak. There is no easy route to the top, so if you want to bag the summit, you should bring a rope and tackle the shallow gully around the corner and up to the right. This is considered somewhere between Class 4 and 5.4.

Route: The peaks of the Buttermilk area are quite visible from downtown Bishop. To get there, turn onto California 168 from US Highway 395 in the center of the town of Bishop and go west about 5 miles. Turn right onto the dirt Buttermilk Road, drive past the Peabody Boulders, and continue up into

Mount Humphreys.

Northeast couloir on Mount Humphrey.

the high desert of the Buttermilk country (7,800'). About a mile past the turn for Basin Mountain, the road reaches a cattle guard and passes through a pretty meadow with aspen trees.

There are nice campsites at the crossing of McGee Creek (high-clearance vehicles recommended). Climb the moraine past the crossing and take the rough road on the right to another junction near a creek gauging station. The road is often impassable, even to four-wheel-drive vehicles, beyond this point. Follow the road or the creek up to the meadow (8,400') below Longley Reservoir.

Follow McGee Creek around the impressive north face of Peaklet to reach the old reservoir (10,700'). From here, climb onto the moraine and into the cirque below the sheer north face of Mount Humphreys. The northeast couloir is the extremely steep gully leading down from the notch (13,600') just north of the peak. After you've tackled the big shot, you can also sample the other gullies dropping down from the Sierra Crest to the north. Finally, to add some extra spice, you can cross the saddle (11,700') between Peaklet and Mount Humphreys and return down the drainage below The Checkered Demon and the Wahoo Gullies to the parking area.

26 Basin Mountain (13,240')

Route:	Basin Couloir
Trailhead:	Buttermilk Road
Vertical:	About 5,000'
Length:	All day
Difficulty:	Class 3
USGS 7.5' Maps:	Mount Tom, Tungsten Hills

Overview: The east couloir on Basin Mountain is one of the premier ski descents in the range. This very long, aesthetic route, which is plainly visible from Bishop, offers great skiing from top to bottom in big snow years. Although it looks quite steep from below, the couloir itself is relatively moderate. The scale of the peak disguises how big the descent really is—the couloir is actually almost 2,500 feet high and over a hundred yards wide. The unique basin on the east side of the peak is huge and the sheer granite cliffs making up the west wall are very impressive. There used to be a mining cabin up in the basin, but it was destroyed by an avalanche. The remains of the old mining road still exist and offer a moderate ascent via long switchbacks up the lower slopes of the peak.

Route: To reach the peak, turn off US Highway 395 in the center of Bishop onto California 168, go west about 5 miles, and then turn right onto the dirt Buttermilk Road. After 3 miles, you'll pass the famous Buttermilk boulders. Continue west, crossing a cattle guard. After another mile, turn right onto

East side of Basin Mountain.

Tom Forsell skiing Basin Mountain.

the road leading to the trailhead for Horton Lakes (8,000'). Late in the season, or in low snow years, you may choose to follow the old mining road into the massive basin midway up the peak. Early in the season, or in bigger snow years, continue on Buttermilk Road until you reach a point even with the southeast toe of the peak, then climb directly up the lower east slopes into the basin. A small glacier and moraine lies at the base of the broad couloir. The couloir itself is surprisingly moderate and there is rarely a cornice at the top. At the col (13,000'), you may wish to leave your skis and climb around to the west ridge and the summit (13,240'). This involves some exposed scrambling. In good years, it is possible to ski from the col all the way out into the sagebrush and almost back to your car.

27 Mount Tom (13,652')

Route: Elderberry Canyon
Trailhead: Rovana
Vertical: About 7,300'
Length: All day
Difficulty: Class 3-4
USGS 7.5' Maps: Mount Tom, Mount Morgan

Overview: This is perhaps the finest peak descent in the entire Sierra. The sweeping line of Elderberry Canyon leading down from the summit of Mount

Elderberry Canyon, Mount Tom.

Tom is a memorable sight to anyone driving south towards Bishop on US Highway 395. Mount Tom is a huge peak, and once you're inside Elderberry Canyon, you'll feel like the canyon walls are the peaks themselves. This run was one of the first Sierra descents to be publicized. In an early edition of the catalog for Chouinard Equipment, long before they began making ski gear or became Black Diamond, there was an essay regarding this peak accompanying their blurb about Salewa Firn skiis—the very short glacier skis popular in Europe at the time.

For most folks, the descent of Elderberry Canyon begins at the old site of Lambert Mine. This makes for a fine, moderate run of close to 4,000 feet. The length of the run obviously depends on the level of the snow line. You'll want to wait until the approach road has melted out, but don't wait too long or the bottom of the gully will be gone. More adventurous skiers may wish to make a descent from the summit of the peak. This involves an extra 2,500 feet of climbing and a reasonably steep descent of the headwall above the mine.

Route: To reach the base of the peak, leave US Highway 395 north of Bishop and travel west on Pine Creek Road to the small mining town of Rovana. The dirt Vanadium Ranch Road leads to the base of the peak (6,300′), where an old mining trail climbs into the canyon. The route climbs over steeper bumps and flats to Lambert Mine (10,850′) in the monstrous cirque at the head of the canyon. For a little extra vertical, you may want to continue to the base of the headwall (11,200′) before heading home. It is possible to climb up the steep headwall (12,350′) to the west and on to the summit (13,652′) via the north ridge. This headwall provides the most challenging skiing on the route. The easiest route is to head north along the ridge before dropping back into the cirque. In any case, you want to begin your run down before the snow gets too soft.

28   Feather Peak (13,242')

Route:	North couloir
Trailhead:	Pine Creek
Vertical:	About 5,500'
Length:	Multiday
Difficulty:	Class 4-5
USGS 7.5' Maps:	Mount Morgan

Overview: Feather Peak is one of the prettiest peaks in the Sierra. The east face is an impressive wall and the north side offers three steep couloirs split by tall granite prows. The south and west ridges are long and wispy with numerous granite towers. The north couloir offers almost 1,200 feet of very steep and exposed skiing from a point just below the summit. The other gullies are shorter, but still worth doing. In 1997, Jim Zellers snowboarded each of these couloirs in an impressive effort. If these runs are beyond your comfort factor, the east couloir between the peak and neighboring Royce Peak is more moderate. Other attractions in the area include the Royce-Merriam Bowl and the run down from Italy Pass through Granite Park.

Granite Park and Feather Peak.

Jim Zellers riding Feather Peak. RICHARD LEVERSEE PHOTO

Route: To get to Pine Creek, leave US Highway 395 north of Bishop and follow Pine Creek Road west past the small mining community of Rovana. The road switchbacks up through a narrow section before straightening out above. Just below the mine, there is a gate and a parking area (7,200'). Follow the summer trail up to Avocet Mine, then take the old dirt road past the obvious avalanche chutes in the vicinity of Brownstone Mine.

North couloir on Feather Peak.

Continue traversing up the canyon to reach Lower Pine Lake (9,950') and then Upper Pine Lake (10,200'). Continue up a series of benches to reach Honeymoon Lake (10,400'). Head for the obvious col (11,700') between the two granite peaks to the south. This col is known as the Co Co La, as the pass lies at the Fresno County/Inyo County boundary and provides access to the Royce Lakes. Feather Peak is to the right; Royce Peak is dead ahead; Merriam Peak is to the left. Skirt the north face of Feather Peak to reach the base of the couloir (12,000) and climb the gully to the summit ridge (13,100'). The summit (13,240') is a short scramble away.

29 Wheeler Crest (13,000')

Route:	Scheelite Chute
Trailhead:	Pine Creek
Vertical:	About 6,000'
Length:	Half day
Difficulty:	Class 4-5
USGS 7.5' Maps:	Mount Morgan

Overview: Wheeler Crest represents perhaps the most impressive fault escarpment along the eastern Sierra, rising 7,000 feet in less than two miles. There are also a number of very attractive couloirs splitting the ramparts of the crest, none more aesthetic than Scheelite Chute. This gully drops in a direct line from the south summit of Broken Finger Peak through the granite portal of Pratts Crack Buttress to the floor of Pine Creek Canyon. You can

Jim Zellers riding Scheelite Chute. Richard Leversee photo

Scheelite Chute, Wheeler Crest.

see the couloir from Bishop, and even though it faces southeast, the gully often holds snow late into the summer. The top of the couloir is very steep and maintains its pitch for a long way. The gully is also deceptively long; from the bottom it looks like about a couple of thousand feet, but it is a full 6,000 feet to the summit. This is also a very serious avalanche path and caution should be taken in all conditions.

Route: To get to Pine Creek, leave US Highway 395 north of Bishop and follow Pine Creek Road west past the small mining community of Rovana. The road becomes steeper as you enter the canyon proper and begins to switchback. Above the switchbacks, the road straightens. On your right, look for the narrow opening of Scheelite Chute about midway up the canyon. A short, dirt road lead up towards the mouth of the canyon, but park near the paved road (7,000') and walk up. The trail passes a popular climbing area before entering the narrow mouth of the canyon at the sharp-cut corner of the famous dihedral of *Pratts Crack*. Continue up the couloir as it gradually gets steeper, finally topping out (13,000') on the south ridge of Broken Finger Peak. The peak's rotten rock makes it difficult and dangerous to traverse to the main summit, and you came for the descent anyway. There's not much else to say; the route is painfully clear from here.

Wheeler Crest and Scheelite Chute.

30 Mount Morgan South (13,748')

Route: Francis Gullies
Trailhead: Rock Creek
Vertical: About 4,800'
Length: Half day
Difficulty: Class 3-4
USGS 7.5' Maps: Mount Morgan

North side of Mount Morgan South.

Overview: Mount Morgan, one of the easiest big peaks to ski in the Sierra, has some of the finest views. This peak is also one of the best to attempt in midwinter. The steep north-facing gullies above Francis Lake provide a very challenging descent, while the ascent route provides a fun run that is a lot more mellow. In the winter, the steep, forested slopes above Kenneth Lake offer excellent powder skiing on the east side. Be aware that this shoulder of the peak is also one of the most frequent avalanche performers and care should be taken.

Route: Take Rock Creek Road off US Highway 395 near Toms Place and continue to the Sno-Park area at East Fork Campground (8,900'). From here, enjoy an easy tour up the groomed road to Rock Creek Lake (9,700'). From the east edge of the lake, follow the marked ski trail east onto the plateau of the East Fork of Rock Creek (10,200'), then climb up the drainage to Kenneth Lake (10,400') and contour south up the steep slopes to an open bench above Francis Lake (11,000'). Follow this natural ski trail towards the obvious gullies before climbing onto the north shoulder (12,500') and on to the summit of Mount Morgan (13,748'). Choose your run back to the bench based on your motivation, skill, and snow conditions. Below the bench, a number of fine powder gullies drop to the meadow at Rock Creek Lodge (9,400'). After stopping for a cold beverage or perhaps dinner and a sauna at the lodge, follow the road or the marked ski trail on the east side of the creek through the woods back to the car.

31 Mount Dade (13,600')

Route: Hourglass Couloir
Trailhead: Rock Creek
Vertical: About 4,700'
Length: All day
Difficulty: Class 3-4
USGS 7.5' Maps: Mount Abbot

Overview: Mount Dade is one of those few peaks that is easier to climb in winter than in summer. Hourglass Couloir provides an excellent ascent route in snowy conditions, and the upper sand slopes are easy to climb on skis. The trip back down is also far more fun on skis than on foot. The upper slopes are moderate and snow coverage is usually more of a problem than pitch, but the angle edges past 40 degrees in the middle of the couloir and the view entering the throat can be somewhat unnerving. Unless the gully is icy, however, the run is very doable by most skiers and the runout is very forgiving. The incredible bowls of the Treasure Lakes lie at the bottom of the run, and they offer excellent midwinter powder and late season corn, with a variety of aspects and slope angles.

Route: Take Rock Creek Road off US Highway 395 near Toms Place and follow it to the Sno-Park area at East Fork Campground (8,900'). From here, tour up the groomed road past Rock Creek Lake (9,700') to the summer parking area at Mosquito Flats (10,200'). Follow the course of Rock Creek

Bear Creek Spire and Hourglass Gully, Mount Dade.

Dave Page skiing below the north ridge of Bear Creek Spire.

up a short hill to Mack Lake (10,350') and Little Lakes Valley. Continue up the drainage passing Marsh, Heart, Box and Long lakes (10,450'), then make a moderate climb up to the Treasure Lakes basin (11,150'). The Saddle Bowl lies between the four lakes and the Practice Slopes are on the southwest margin of the basin. Hourglass Couloir lies directly south of the lakes and leads to the upper slopes and summit of Mount Dade (13,600'). There is a great view from the top.

32 Mount Abbot (13,715')

Route: North couloir
Trailhead: Rock Creek
Vertical: About 4,700'
Length: All day
Difficulty: Class 4
USGS 7.5' Maps: Mount Abbot

Overview: Mount Abbot is a very popular peak with mountaineers due to its height, position, and difficulty. There are no easy routes to the top; however, in late spring and early summer, the north couloir provides a very fine descent from just below the summit. The top is quite steep, but the gully is such that you can bail out on the climb at any point and just turn around for the schuss back down. There is another fine gully just to the west that leads to a notch between Mount Abbot and Mount Mills below the prominent granite spire known as The Petite Griffon. This gully affords the advantage of a flat col for putting on your skis and summoning your nerve. Either run is steep enough to be interesting, but not suicidal.

North face of Mount Abbot from Mills Lake.

Route: Take Rock Creek Road off US Highway 395 near Toms Place and follow it to the Sno-Park area at East Fork Campground (8,900'). From here, tour up the groomed road past Rock Creek Lake (9,700') to the summer parking area at Mosquito Flats (10,200'). Climb the first hill above the flats, then follow the outlet creek of Ruby Lake up and to the right to Ruby Lake (11,100'). Continue south up the valley past Mills Lake (11,600') and on to the glacier below the peak (12,200'). If you are trying to gain the summit of Mount Abbot (13,704'), the best route breaks to the right of the gully about midway up (leave your skis there) and attains the narrow west ridge. Otherwise, keep going straight up the obvious gully until you get your fill. The direct route to the summit plateau is blocked by a difficult chimney. As an alternative, you may want to sample the neighboring couloir leading to the col between The Petite Griffon and Mount Mills.

33 Mount Starr (12,832')

Route:	East gullies
Trailhead:	Rock Creek Lake
Vertical:	About 4,000'
Length:	A few hours
Difficulty:	Class 3-4
USGS 7.5' Maps:	Mount Abbot

Overview: Mount Starr is another fine ski peak that has little attraction for the summer mountaineer. The gullies on the east side of Mount Starr are very similar to those of neighboring Pointless Peak. They offer long runs at a consistent pitch and serious avalanche hazard under most conditions. In 1986, most of the gullies released and took out huge swaths of forest. There is often a large cornice lurking over the middle gully. The gully directly above Mosquito Flats is steeper and features a couple of small cliff bands to keep things interesting. Overall, it's best to wait until spring or very stable conditions to tackle this peak. The entire north slope of the peak offers good skiing (also with major league "avie" hazard), and there are two very steep couloirs breaching the cliffs just south of Half Moon Pass that are worth checking out. The south side of the peak has a fine, broad gully dropping down to Ruby Lake, and the run down from Mono Pass on the southwest side is worthwhile, too.

Route: Mount Starr looms over the road between Rock Creek Lake and Mosquito Flats. Take the Rock Creek Road off US Highway 395 near Toms Place and follow it to the Sno-Park area at East Fork Campground (8,900'). From here, follow an easy, 3-mile groomed road, courtesy of the folks at Rock Creek Lodge. Continue past Rock Creek Lake (9,700') and turn west at the summer pack station to reach the north bowl. To reach the first gullies leading off the east side of the summit ridge, head west from Mosquito Flats Campground. There are gullies all along the slope facing the road. The summit of the peak (12,835') is located near the south end of the summit ridge.

Dave Page skiing Mount Starr.

East gullies on Mount Starr.

A steep gully drops down from the top to the end of the road at Mosquito Flats. To reach Mono Pass and the south side, follow the outlet creek to Ruby Lake (11,100') and contour around to the west. Just about any route you pick is worthwhile.

34 Pointless Peak (12,252')

Route: Y Gullies
Trailhead: Rock Creek Lake
Vertical: About 3,300'
Length: A few hours
Difficulty: Class 3-4
USGS 7.5' Maps: Mount Abbot

Overview: As with Mount Locke, Pointless Peak is one of the finest secret ski peaks in the range. Some Rock Creek locals have been known to make daily pilgrimages up the peak in spring. The name Pointless Peak was derived from the fact that the top is a very broad plateau and the summit is merely a pile of rocks on the high end of the plain. The name also comes from locals trying to mislead visiting skiers, "Why, it's pointless to go up there." Despite their efforts, the Y Gullies that grace the east face provide excellent challenges for skilled skiers and boarders. Please note that these branching gullies (they form a series of Y's) are prime avalanche paths and

166

Dave Page making pedal turns on Mount Starr.

East gullies on Pointless Peak.

snowslides have occasionally run all the way to the road. As a result, these runs should only be attempted under very stable conditions.

A trio of excellent gullies drops from the summit, following a twisting course before merging at the avalanche cones at the base of the peak. On the north side of the peak is Patricia Bowl, home of some of the finest powder skiing in the range. The south slopes empty into Half Moon Bowl, which offers a broad variety of runs. Any way you go, you're bound to have fun, otherwise, it would all be pointless.

Route: Pointless Peak is plainly visible from Rock Creek Lake. Take Rock Creek Road off US Highway 395 near Toms Place and continue to the Sno-Park area at East Fork Campground (8,900'). From here, follow an easy, 3-mile groomed road to the lake (9,700'). From the pack station above the lake, head west onto the obvious avalanche cone and ascend your chosen gully. The summit of the peak (12,252') is at the northeast edge of the summit plateau. The impressive drop to the north ends in Patricia Bowl. Perhaps some future suicidal extreme skier will find a way through these cliffs. Otherwise, you can get to the bowl by contouring north along the base of the peak. To reach Half Moon Bowl, contour south along the base of the peak.

35 Mount Morgan North (13,005')

Route: Nevahbe Ridge gullies
Trailhead: Hilton Creek
Vertical: About 5,000'
Length: Half day
Difficulty: Class 3-4
USGS 7.5' Maps: Convict Lake

Overview: On the east side of the Nevahbe Ridge, there are several very attractive avalanche chutes. This ridge forms a dramatic backdrop for the small community of Hilton Lake and provides a private playground for local residents. An old mining road skirts the base of the ridge and provides access to the chutes. The most prominent of the gullies, which drops from a point just north of the summit of the peak, is one of the longest, continuously steep runs in the eastern Sierra. These chutes are very frequent avalanche performers, so be prepared. Around to the east, a broad couloir drops from the summit of the peak down toward Davis Lake and is known as the Grand Central Couloir. All of these routes put significant air beneath your ski tips as you drop in.

Route: To reach the trailhead, turn south off US Highway 395 onto Old Highway 395 (Crowley Lake Drive) and head west towards McGee Creek. Turn south again onto the dirt road accessing the BLM campground (7,000')

Nevahbe Ridge, Mount Morgan North.

169

and follow this up as high as you can go toward the base of the ridge (8,000'). Continue on foot until you find the gully of your dreams and follow it uphill forever. Once on top of the ridge (12,550'), return the way you came, continue on to the summit (13,005'), or drop down the west side into Esha Canyon. If you continue up the old road towards Davis Lake, you will pass some abandoned mine workings and then, eventually, the Hilton Creek Mine. Although the gold never panned out, this ridge still offers a treasure trove of fine descents.

36 Esha Peak (12,800')

Route:	Esha Canyon
Trailhead:	McGee Creek
Vertical:	About 5,000'
Length:	Half day
Difficulty:	Class 3-4
USGS 7.5' Maps:	Convict Lake

Overview: This descent has long been a local favorite because it provides a great run down a wonderful, hidden canyon close to the road. It actually descends a subsidiary peak from Mount Morgan North, on the west side of Esha Canyon. The peak looks like a cousin of Mount Locke, with five gullies extending like fingers through the cliffs. As with Wahoo Gully, the run takes

Mount Morgan North and Esha Canyon.

Mount McGee and Esha Canyon.

an aesthetic line down the middle finger, then follows the roller-coaster ride of the lower Esha Canyon.

Route: To reach the trailhead, turn west off US Highway 395 onto McGee Creek Road. This road skirts the base of Mount McGee before climbing the moraine and accessing the canyon. Much of the route up Esha Canyon is protected from view by the very colorful Nevahbe Ridge. Park just below the McGee Creek Pack Station (7,700') and cross the creek (may be difficult in high water); then climb up into the hanging valley to the south. The ascent follows a series of steep benches toward the head of the north-facing cirque. From here, there are a number of options. A moderately steep slope heads up and left to the huge plateau just below the summit of Mount Morgan North (13,005'). Steeper descents are available down the north slope of Nevahbe Ridge, as well as down the east gullies dropping off Nevahbe Ridge into the drainage of Hilton Creek. The main run of Esha Canyon takes the very steep central gully on the northeast face of the pyramid peak (12,800'), which looms over the west side of the canyon. From the small lake about halfway up the canyon, climb directly up the gully. Once on top, enjoy the view, then try to hold it all together for the steep descent back into the canyon.

37 Mount McGee (10,871')

Route: 395 gullies
Trailhead: US Highway 395
Vertical: About 3,200'
Length: A few hours
Difficulty: Class 3
USGS 7.5' Maps: Convict Lake

Overview: Mount McGee was the site of one of the first ski areas in the eastern Sierra. The rope tow operation situated at the base of these gullies eventually was moved and became Mammoth Mountain. Mammoth Heli-Ski also used to visit Mount McGee in the spring with $25 local runs. These gullies are still very popular and provide a classic roadside attraction above US Highway 395 near Crowley Lake. The central, northeast facing gullies are the most popular, but there are very skiable runs down the northwest and southeast sides as well. Because the summit is not in the wilderness, it is possible to access these runs via snowmobile. This means you may have to share the slopes with folks making multiple runs, but there's room for all. Be aware that these are all very active avalanche paths and should only be attempted during periods of low hazard.

Route: Runs don't get much more obvious than this. From US Highway 395 just north of Crowley Lake, turn west onto Old Highway 395 (Crowley Lake

Northeast gullies on Mount McGee.

Drive) at either the McGee or Long Valley exits. Follow Old Highway 395 to a stone monument on the side of the road at the base of the main gully, noting the original rope tow site. Climb straight up the shallow gully leading from the monument (6,900') toward the summit ridge and on to the summit (10,900'). As an alternative, the avalanche path dropping directly from the summit toward the trailer park is also good. For this run, drive up McGee Creek Road a short distance and park on the old mining road leading toward the peak. Another fine route is found at the northwest end of Old Highway 395 spur, just above the houses at Long Valley. Either climb the gully or detour around to the west and up the west flank of the peak from Tobacco Flats. There are a number of other fun gullies on this side of the peak as well.

38 Mount Morrison (12,268')

Route: Old Man's Bowl
Trailhead: Convict Lake
Vertical: About 4,500'
Length: Half day
Difficulty: Class 3-4
USGS 7.5' Maps: Bloody Mountain, Convict Lake

Overview: Mount Morrison is one of the most spectacular peaks anywhere. The sheer north face of the peak is very enticing, but the rotten rock will deter all but the most suicidal climbers. It would seem that only the most suicidal skier would attempt a route on this side of the peak, but apparently the narrow gully to the west of the north face (called Death Couloir by Doug Robinson and Yvon Chouinard) has been skied at least once. Conditions allowing such a descent are extremely rare and involve ice climbing more than skiing. The east side of the peak has the best descent routes, and the classic Old Man's Bowl is the best of the best even though it does not take you to the top of the peak. This run drops from the subsidiary peak north of Mount Morrison known as Black Mountain (11,108'). Heading up the valley above Tobacco Flat, the bowl is not visible until you almost reach the base. Mammoth Heli-Ski used to frequent this run, too.

Route: The ascent route begins at Convict Lake (7,600'). To reach the lake, turn west on Convict Lake Road off US Highway 395 opposite Mammoth Lakes Airport. Head east from the campground at the lake to reach the top of the moraine. Soon you'll reach the upper part of Tobacco Flats and the east fork of Convict Creek drainage. Follow the broad moraine up the center of the valley to avoid the runout zones of the major "avie" paths off the north side of the north summit of Black Mountain (also called Little Morrison). Continue around Black Mountain to reach the base of Old Man's Bowl;

Old Man's Bowl, Mount Morrison.

then climb the bowl to the summit of Black Mountain on the left (11,108'). Return the way you came. As an alternative, you can make a loop by dropping into the hanging valley below the impressive east face of Mount Morrison. Death Couloir lies tucked away in this drainage. Also, the east slopes of the higher summit of Mount Morrison can be skied from near the summit. Finally, check out the Hand Gullies on nearby Mount Aggie, as well as the narrow gully on the shoulder of the large, square peak at the head of the canyon.

39 Red Slate Mountain (13,163')

Route:	North couloir
Trailhead:	Convict Lake
Vertical:	About 5,600'
Length:	All day (or multiday)
Difficulty:	Class 5
USGS 7.5' Maps:	Bloody Mountain, Convict Lake

Overview: Convict Canyon is one of the most unique locations in the Sierra. The very colorful, folded cliffs of Mount Morrison, Laurel Mountain, and Mount Baldwin are composed of the oldest rock in the range. The north couloir of the peak is very impressive, but due to its somewhat hidden position, the gully is not as well known as some of its neighbors. However, the view of the peak from the top of Bloody Couloir is enough to make any extreme skier add an extra day or two to his vacation. This descent is not for the faint of heart by any means. Just getting in can involve passing a big cornice with almost 2,000 feet of air below you. Beyond the cornice, a short jog to skier's left above a cliff is required to access the gully proper. Once in the main couloir, the fall line has a nasty habit of taking you into the wall of the gully, so don't fall. I don't know who was the first to ski this line, but Kevin Kleinfelter made the first Nordic descent in the early 1980s. Note that while Kevin made a clean run, his partner (to remain nameless) fell and broke his leg. You've been warned.

Route: To access the approach to Red Slate Mountain, leave US Highway 395 near Mammoth Lakes Airport and turn onto Convict Lake Road. At Convict Lake (7,600'), follow the summer trail around the base of Laurel Mountain and into the dark depths of Convict Canyon. Entering the mouth of the canyon, you pass a very interesting hidden couloir to the west before reaching a ghost forest on the canyon floor. Then follow the creek through a narrow cleft past the twisted remains of a bridge that was damaged by an avalanche (9,000'). Sinister black towers guard the entrance to the canyon, like something out of Tolkien. The canyon remains very claustrophobic for a way before suddenly opening up at Mildred Lake (9,800'). Either climb the couloir itself, or take the more moderate west slopes to the summit (13,163'). Before you tackle the couloir, make sure your skills are up to the task, because this is one place that a lost edge could kill you. If the gully is

North couloir on Red Slate Mountain.

too spooky, the west slopes provide a long, fun run down. There are also some nice gullies on the northeast slopes of the peak. The run down Convict Creek is like a long half pipe—a great trip in its own right.

40 Laurel Mountain (11,812')

Route: Mendenhall Couloir
Trailhead: Convict Lake
Vertical: About 4,200'
Length: Half day
Difficulty: Class 5
USGS 7.5' Maps: Bloody Mountain

Overview: The central gully on the colorful northeast face of Laurel Mountain is one of the most attractive and challenging descents in the eastern Sierra. This route has an interesting history. It was quite likely the site of the first properly belayed climb in the Sierra when John Mendenhall and his partner climbed it in 1930. Driving north on US Highway 395 towards Mammoth Lakes Airport, this impressive line is very obvious as you pass a church, locally known as the "green church." The crux of the route lies in the tremendous exposure beneath your feet as you drop in. Other difficulties include various ice or rock cliffs that must be negotiated in the narrow middle section of the couloir. This gully is the frequent site of massive winter

Mendenhall Couloir, Laurel Mountain.

avalanches, and it is a rare year when the entire couloir has good conditions and enough snow to allow a reasonably safe descent.

Route: Convict Lake Road is opposite Mammoth Lakes Airport on US Highway 395. Turn left on this road and follow it up to the spectacular trailhead at Convict Lake. The lake is bordered by the impressive north face of Mount Morrison and the northeast face and Sevehah Cliffs of Laurel Mountain. The gully begins a short distance south of Convict Lake (7,600′). Follow the summer trail to the obvious runout zone and climb the gully. There are a couple of very steep steps that will likely be icy, and crampons and ice axes are definitely a must. The gully broadens out into a very steep bowl at the top; you may have to exit right to avoid the large cornice that often forms near the summit (11,812′).

On the summit, summon your courage, drop in where you can, and hang on for dear life. This descent is only for the very skilled and may require a few sections of downclimbing or roped skiing to be handled safely. Good luck. The bottom third is a worthwhile descent in its own right and avoids the extreme sections higher up. There is also another sick couloir just on the other side of the ridge of Sevehah Cliffs. Continue up Convict Canyon about a half mile farther and you will see the bottom of the gully. This shot is very narrow and quite steep at the top. Cool.

41 Bloody Mountain (12,544′)

Route:	Bloody Couloir
Trailhead:	Laurel Lakes Road
Vertical:	About 4,000′
Length:	Half day
Difficulty:	Class 4-5
USGS 7.5′ Maps:	Bloody Mountain

Overview: Driving into the town of Mammoth Lakes, especially from the north, the dark slot of Bloody Couloir looms ominously above the road. This is probably the locals' premier extreme ski descent, and the area is skied quite often, even in the middle of winter. The name Bloody comes from the red rock of the peak, rather than some gruesome historical event. However, during periods of warm weather, the rockfall from the sides of the couloir could definitely put a dent in your balaclava. Once you get close, you'll see that there are actually parallel gullies separated by two prominent rock islands. The true Bloody Couloir drops from the west summit on the skier's left and takes a route on the left side of the top island. It is quite steep in the upper pitch. Alternatively, the gully on the skier's right offers a straighter shot from the main summit, and although it's not quite as steep, it offers a better fall line descent.

North side of Bloody Mountain.

Route: The access to Bloody Mountain begins off US Highway 395 at Sherwin Creek Road. Follow this dirt road for about 2 miles until you reach the junction with the four-wheel-drive road to Laurel Lakes. Alternatively, if you come from the town of Mammoth Lakes, turn onto Sherwin Creek Road from Old Mammoth Road and follow it past the Sherwin Creek Campground and the Los Angeles YMCA camp to the turnoff for Laurel Lakes Road. Follow the very steep and rutted road (high-clearance four-wheel-drive mandatory) up the moraine to the pretty meadow (8,400') below Laurel Lakes. The road continues climbing in two giant switchbacks, but driving much beyond the meadow is not recommended. Park your car in a safe place (away from any rockfall/avalanche path) and walk up the road toward Laurel Lakes, passing the Laurel/Bloody Bowl before contouring around to reach the open slope at the base of the couloir.

There are many options from here. The Y-shaped gullies to the left offer extremely steep and challenging descents. The main couloir is split by two prominent rock towers. The best ascent route is along the left side of the towers, which also provides the best fall line descent. The main Bloody Couloir drops very steeply from the summit (12,544') on the left (west) side of the high tower before joining the other route on the right (east) side of the lower tower. The gully dropping down the left (west) side of the lower tower also offers good skiing. Another fine descent is via the parallel gullies draining into the Laurel/Bloody Bowl from the east ridge of the peak. Finally, the south face offers a great run into Convict Canyon. All in all, this is one of the finest Sierra ski peaks.

Dropping in on Bloody Mountain.

42　Pyramid Peak (11,728')

Route: Para Chute Couloir
Trailhead: Laurel Lakes Road
Vertical: About 3,300'
Length: Half day
Difficulty: Class 5
USGS 7.5' Maps: Bloody Mountain

Overview: You can see this impressive couloir from Mammoth Lakes Airport. Longtime local climber and skier Walt Rosenthal made the first descent in the early 1980s. He called it the Para Chute in recognition of the unrelenting pitch of the couloir. Dropping in from the top of the chute is like dropping out of an airplane. You better hope your chute opens or you'll have a rough landing at the bottom. The gully begins at the notch between the twin summits of Pyramid Peak above the Sherwins. The couloir takes a deep gash in the cliffs on the east side of the peak. Although it is possible to rappel in to the top of the gully from the summit, most intelligent skiers will climb the thing from the bottom to check conditions first. The bowl to the south of the couloir is also worth checking out.

Route: The best access to the east side of Pyramid Peak follows the approach to Bloody Mountain. Begin at US Highway 395 and turn west onto Sherwin Creek Road. Follow this dirt road for about 2 miles until you reach the junction with the four-wheel-drive Laurel Lakes Road. Alternatively, if

Para Chute, Pyramid Peak.

Jim Zellers riding Para Chute. RICHARD LEVERSEE PHOTO

you come from the town of Mammoth Lakes, turn onto Sherwin Creek Road from Old Mammoth Road and follow it past the Sherwin Creek Campground and the Los Angeles YMCA camp to the turnoff for Laurel Lakes Road. Follow the very steep and rutted road (high-clearance four-wheel-drive mandatory) up the moraine to the pretty meadow (8,400') below Laurel Lakes. Park here and cross the moraine to the southwest to reach Valentine Creek at Lost Lakes (9,000'). Continue southwest into the cirque below the peak and cross the moraine to reach the base of the couloir. Climb this to the top (11,728') and pull the ripcord.

43 The Sherwins (10,166')

Route:	Avie Path (Dempsey Don't)
Trailhead:	Twin Lakes/Tamarack Lodge
Vertical:	About 2,200'
Length:	A few hours
Difficulty:	Class 3
USGS 7.5' Maps:	Bloody Mountain, Crystal Crag

Overview: To backcountry skiers, The Sherwins is like a candy store. This easily accessed area is extremely popular and offers a full range of backcountry skiing opportunities. The Sherwins is bounded on the east by the prominent ridge known as Punta Bardini, named in honor of longtime local guide Allan Bard. This steep ridgeline offers a number of active avalanche paths and open tree runs. At the base of Punta Bardini, there are two open shots in the trees known as the Tele Bowls. These bowls, as well as Solitude Canyon, are best approached from the Sierra Meadows Touring Center on Old Mammoth Road.

The main feature of The Sherwins is the broad avalanche path that ends near Hidden Lake. A massive avalanche in February 1986 wiped out a huge section of mature forest. To the east of the "avie" path, there is an open bowl with a series of short gullies known as The Fingers. Rock Chute splits the cliffs on the east side of this bowl. Dropping into the throat of this steep gully is a rite of passage into the ranks of the local extreme community.

To the west of the avalanche path, there is a narrow, tree-lined gully known as The Hose. To the right of The Hose, there is another avalanche path and open tree skiing below the ridge. Easter Bowl lies directly above the prominent Mammoth Rock. Two very narrow gullies (known as The Poop Chutes) provide routes past Mammoth Rock and onto the steep apron below. Finally, The Mineshaft is a steep chute through the red cliffs above the old mining campsite near Lake Mary Road. Please note that all of these runs are obviously exposed to very high avalanche hazard and should be skied with great caution under nothing but the most stable conditions.

John Moynier skiing the main "avie" path, The Sherwins.

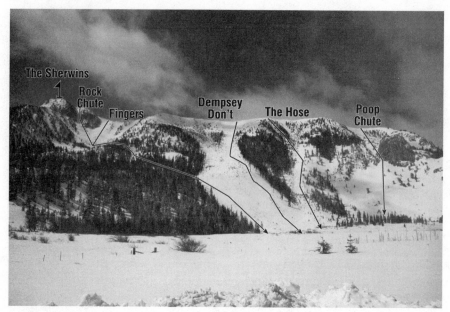

Main section of The Sherwins.

Route: The runs on the main ridge of The Sherwins are most easily accessed from Twin Lakes (8,700'). To get there, turn onto California 203 off US Highway 395 and drive through the town of Mammoth Lakes to the end of the plowed road at Twin Lakes. You can do a shuttle by leaving a car at Snowcreek Golf Course at the base (8,000'). Ski up the road (staying out of the groomed tracks of Tamarack Lodge) to just past the junction with Old Mammoth Road. From here, a boot trail usually leads past a mine (still active) to the base of the cliffs on the ridge. A short chute leads through the cliffs and onto the broad plateau (10,100') at the top. From the top, walk out the windswept plateau until you reach the top of your desired descent. Most of these runs finish near Hidden Lake, which lies at the bottom of the big avalanche path. A final skate across Snowcreek Golf Course allows access to Ranch Road.

44 Mammoth Crest (11,348')

Route:	The Crest Shots
Trailhead:	Twin Lakes/Tamarack Lodge
Vertical:	About 3,000'
Length:	Half day
Difficulty:	Class 3-4
USGS 7.5' Maps:	Bloody Mountain, Crystal Crag

Overview: The high bowls and couloirs of Mammoth Crest offer excellent powder skiing in the winter, as well as perhaps the best summer skiing in the eastern Sierra. It is easy to see this ridge from the top of Mammoth Mountain, as well as from the parking area at Twin Lakes near Tamarack Lodge. The crest begins at the low saddle of Mammoth Pass (9,300') and quickly rises south in a series of cliffs. The narrow shot of Hollywood Bowl splits these cliffs and provides a run down to McLeod Lake and the pass. One of the most popular runs in the Mammoth area is Red Cone Bowl (10,600'), which is located on the volcanic crest between McLeod Lake and Crystal Lake. It is best to approach this section of the crest either from Horseshoe Lake and Mammoth Pass, or from Lake George and the summer trail to Crystal Lake. Both of these routes follow forested ridgelines that are fairly free of avalanche hazard.

The section of the crest above Crystal Lake is dominated by a huge cornice known as Jaws. There are a number of short, steep gullies splitting the cliffs here like The Dogleg Couloir and The Echo Chamber. The moderate basin just above TJ Lake (9,250') is known as The Child's Play Bowl. The top part of this bowl is rather steep and subject to frequent avalanches. Above and left of this bowl, there are numerous bowls and chutes along the Mammoth Crest (11,200').

Farther south, the most prominent feature on the crest is a large granite buttress called The Ship's Prow. The bowl just right of the prow offers excellent skiing down to scenic Hammil Lake (10,000'), and there are several fine couloirs in the area. It is best to access this section from Coldwater Campground via the route up Coldwater Creek. Farther south on the crest, locate the obvious Blue Crag, with popular Blue Couloir on the left and

The Ship's Prow, Mammoth Crest.

185

John Moynier skiing on Mammoth Crest. KELLY VAN DUSEN PHOTO

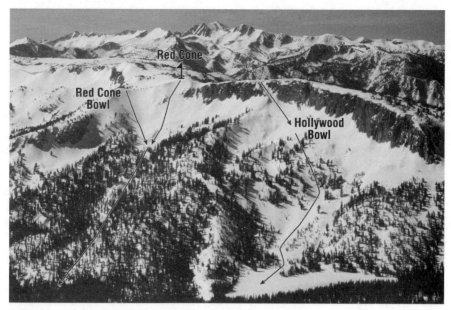

Red Cones area, Mammoth Crest with Silver Divide in background.

narrow Crag Couloir on the right. Finally, just before Duck Pass, the bowls above Barney Lake (10,250') also offer fine spring skiing. These areas can be reached by following either Coldwater or Mammoth creeks.

Route: In the winter, it is easiest to access Mammoth Crest from Twin Lakes (8,700'). To get there, turn onto California 203 off US Highway 395 and drive through the town of Mammoth Lakes to the end of the plowed road at Twin Lakes. Ski up the groomed Lake Mary Road (stay out of the tracks please) to Lake Mary (8,900'). Turn right to reach Horseshoe Lake and Mammoth Pass. Turn left to reach the trailhead for Coldwater and The Ship's Prow and Duck Pass areas. Continue up the road to Lake George (9,000') to reach the Red Cone, Jaws, and TJ Lake areas.

45 Mount Ritter (13,157')

Route: Ediza Couloir
Trailhead: Agnew Meadows
Vertical: About 5,000'
Length: Multiday
Difficulty: Class 3-4
USGS 7.5' Maps: Mount Ritter

Overview: Mount Ritter is a very popular ski peak in the spring and can be done in a day after the Devils Postpile Road opens (although the descent will be shorter).

Southeast side of Mount Ritter.

If the road is not open, this run becomes more like a 3-day trip or longer. As such, most folks set up a base camp in the Ediza Lake area and enjoy the high country around The Minarets before the pesky summer mosquitos wake up. Most of the descent is quite moderate, with the exception of the narrow couloir midway up that breaks through a prominent cliff band. Another good objective in the area is the large bowl located between Mount Ritter and Banner Peak to the north. In some years, it is possible to ski most of the south slope of Banner Peak from the summit. This is pretty steep, though, so be prepared.

Route: It is best to access Mount Ritter from the Mammoth Mountain Ski Area and Devils Postpile Road. To get there, turn west onto California 203 off US Highway 395 and drive through the town of Mammoth Lakes. Follow the signs to the ski area. You may have to take the shuttle in the winter to avoid parking problems. Take Devils Postpile Road over Minaret Summit to the Agnew Meadows Campground (8,600'), then follow the summer trail down to the bridge on the Middle Fork of the San Joaquin River (8,100') before climbing back up to Shadow Lake (8,700'). From here, follow Shadow Creek up to Lake Ediza (9,250'), and then follow the drainage to the west up to the small glacier on the south side of the peak. From here, a steep gully leads to the summit slopes and the top (13,157'). There is a tremendous view of The Minarets as well as the southern part of Yosemite National Park from the top. The broad summit snowfield funnels down to the very steep couloir before regaining the open bowl back to Ediza Lake and the drainage leading to Shadow Lake. If you are making this trip as an overnighter, you might want to detour up Volcanic Ridge (11,400') for a run down the north avalanche gullies. There is a really fine view of The Minarets and the rest of the Ritter Range from the summit.

46 San Joaquin Mountain (11,600')

Route: The Negatives
Trailhead: June Lake Loop
Vertical: About 4,200'
Length: Half day
Difficulty: Class 4
USGS 7.5' Maps: Mammoth Mountain, June Lake

Overview: San Joaquin Mountain is another peak that offers a wide range of descent possibilities. In the spring, the southeast slopes offer a wonderful corn run down into the Glass Creek drainage. In the winter, the north slopes offer prime powder skiing down to Fern Lake, with the option of a finish down the unique Devils Slide. However, for most folks the main attraction on the peak is the series of gullies leading off the northeast side of the east peak. These gullies, which are very obvious from the nearby June Mountain Ski Area, are collectively referred to as The Negatives. These steep gullies empty into a very nice bowl just west of the ski area boundary, and with a little forethought (and the assistance of the ski area), you can use lift access to shorten the journey. Otherwise, access is via the Fern Lake or Yost Creek trails.

Route: From US Highway 395, drive west on the June Lake Loop (California 158) to the June Mountain Ski Area (6,400'). If you are using the lifts, head to the top of June Mountain (10,100'), then descend west to the saddle

The Negatives, San Joaquin Mountain.

The author skiing in the Mammoth area.

(9,700') between June Mountain and San Joaquin Mountain. If you are hoofing it, continue on the June Lake Loop to the trailhead for the Yost Creek Trail (7,300'). Follow the basic course of the trail up the steep, forested slope to the valley above, then follow the creek past Yost Lake and up to the saddle.

From the saddle, head west up a short, steep slope to reach the broad expanses on the southeast side of the peak. Keep to the right to reach the east peak (11,200') and the top of The Negatives. The run you pick will depend on snow conditions and your motivation. These gullies all face more or less east and converge in the large bowl below. This is a very dangerous place during periods of high avalanche hazard. Be prepared, and use as much caution as you can. If things are too dicey, you can always return the way you came and head out the Yost Creek drainage or back to the ski area.

A very popular run in its own right is the trip down the north side of the peak to Fern Lake and down Devils Slide. From the saddle between the summits of the peak, head north down an increasingly steep bowl. Stay in the middle of the drainage to avoid cliffs, then hold a high traverse above the lake before climbing over the low ridge to access Devils Slide. Check out the Carson Peak description (below) for details on playing on the Slide.

47 Carson Peak (10,909')

> **Route:** Northeast face to Devils Slide
> **Trailhead:** June Lake Loop
> **Vertical:** About 3,500'
> **Length:** Half day
> **Difficulty:** Class 4
> **USGS 7.5' Maps:** Mammoth Mountain, June Lake

Overview: Carson Peak has long been a popular ski descent with the locals. In fact, there were a number of races held down the central bowl before World War II. The lower gully, known as Devils Slide, is very prominent from the June Lake Loop near Silver Lake. The upper bowls are in plain sight from US Highway 395, as well as the slopes of nearby June Mountain Ski Area. The tricky part of the descent comes when you try to connect the upper and lower sections. The best route follows ledges fairly high above the beginning of Devils Slide. Things could get ugly if you drop too low, and you really don't want to lose an edge and enter the gully with a 150-foot tumble over the cliffs. It's bad form and you'd miss the fine turns in the upper part of the gully.

Devils Slide, a perfect natural half pipe, is a popular run in its own right, especially with snowboarders. The north face of the peak has also been skied and offers a much more serious adventure known as Pete's Dream, in honor of longtime local Pete Schoerner, who made the first descent. Pete

North face of Carson Peak.

was killed in a tragic ice-climbing accident nearby in 1995. The run averages over 45 degrees for more than 2,000 feet and serves as a fitting memorial and testament to his boldness and skill.

Route: From US Highway 395, drive west on June Lake Loop (California 158), passing the June Mountain Ski Area and the Carson Peak Inn. Just past the summer parking for the Fern Lake Trail, there is a huge mansion on the right. A broad street leads toward the peak on the left. Park off the pavement and keep a respectful distance from the houses at the end of the street (7,300'). Pass through a short stretch of woods (some minor creek crossings) to access the obvious avalanche runout zone at the base of the Slide. Ascend the gully as it gently gets steeper to reach the shoulder of the peak at the top of the Slide (9,200').

From here, climb up and to the right on snowy ledges to reach the base of the upper bowl. You may want to mark the point so you can find it again on the descent. Climb the bowl on the left side and exit onto the flat summit ridge (10,900'). Be aware that the top of the bowl is often guarded by a huge cornice, and this can make things considerably more interesting. You should be able to ski all the way back to the car. Just don't forget to cut right on the descent to safely reach the top of Devils Slide (or you will really wish you had said your prayers the night before). Once in the gully itself, tear it up. To reach Pete's Dream, head out the summit ridge all of the way to the north and decide if your life is worth the risk.

48 Mount Wood (12,637')

Route: East gullies
Trailhead: Silver Lake
Vertical: About 5,500'
Length: Half day
Difficulty: Class 3-4
USGS 7.5' Maps: Koip Peak, June Lake

Overview: This descent is another of the great east side giants, and these gullies dominate the view from US Highway 395 north of June Lake Junction. If you catch it right, you can hike up the sunny south-facing trail from Silver Lake to the bench at 9,000 feet before putting on your skis. Most of the descent is quite moderate, but the top 1,000 feet or so is pretty steep. After bagging the big descent, you can finish off your leg by skiing down to the road at Grant Lake. You'll have to leave a shuttle car or stash a bike over there, though, unless you want to walk or hitchhike back to the car.

Route: To reach the trailhead at Silver Lake, turn west onto California 158 at June Lake Junction and follow this road through town and past the ski area to Silver Lake (7,200'). Follow the summer trail up onto the broad bench (9,000') at the eastern foot of the peak. It is possible to reach the bench from the trailhead for Parker Lake (7,800') when the north end of the June Lake Loop is opened in the spring. From the bench, you have several options to reach the summit. Either climb straight up the central couloir or take the

East face of Mount Wood.

more moderate gully to the left that accesses the south ridge of the peak. You should follow whichever route you plan to descend from the summit (12,650').

Once on top, you have fine views of Mono Lake, as well as the headwaters of Rush Creek and the northern end of the Ritter Range. The main gully drops straight down from the summit through the cliffs to the bench and offers the most aesthetic descent. The southeast bowls offer a more moderate descent. Some folks, however, may choose to enjoy a couple of runs on the great east slope below the cliffs (11,000') and not even bother going to the summit. To ski down to Grant Lake, take the steep, aspen-filled gully just north of the dome (9,200') on the eastern edge of the bench and drop down to the road.

49 Mount Gibbs (12,764')

Route:	Walker gullies
Trailhead:	Walker Lake
Vertical:	About 4,500'
Length:	Half day
Difficulty:	Class 3-4
USGS 7.5' Maps:	Mount Dana

Overview: Mount Gibbs, located just southeast of Mount Dana, is a very interesting peak. The northeast summit sits on the ridge between Mount

Northeast gullies on Mount Gibbs.

194

Gibbs and Mount Dana at the head of a great cirque. The run down the north glacier in Gibbs Canyon past Kidney Lake and Gibbs Lake to the Lee Vining Campground is another of the giant descents of the eastern Sierra. Our route, however, takes the prominent avalanche paths on the eastern slopes of the peak above Walker Lake. Although you can see the route clearly from US Highway 395 between June Lake and Lee Vining, the peak has a fairly remote feel, and the evidence of frequent large avalanches necessitates extra caution. These very steep avalanche gullies are quite similar to those on their neighbor, Mount Wood, only steeper. The west slopes leading down the Dana Fork of the Tuolumne River to Dana Meadows and Tioga Pass are also popular.

Route: To reach the trailhead at Walker Lake (7,950'), turn west off US Highway 395 just south of Lee Vining onto the marked dirt road leading to the lake. This road can also be reached from the north end of June Lake Loop (California 158). Follow the road to the lake, then climb directly up your chosen slope to the northeast summit of the peak (12,565'). Descents of the north side begin at Lee Vining Campground, while it is best to access the west slope of the peak from Tioga Pass. It is also possible to use a car shuttle at Tioga Pass to access the summits of Mount Gibbs. This nice tour cuts off a fair amount of climbing but does not give you the confidence of checking out conditions on the approach.

50 Mount Dana (13,053')

Route: Dana Couloir
Trailheads: Tioga Pass and Ellery Lake
Vertical: About 3,000'
Length: Half day
Difficulty: Class 4
USGS 7.5' Maps: Mount Dana

Overview: This classic springtime ritual can be a bit crowded, especially over the Memorial Day weekend when you actually might see someone else. If you catch this descent early in the season, just after the road opens, you can ski all the way. The Fun Hog way to do this is to finish with one of the gullies in the Ellery Bowl. You'll need a car shuttle or to hitchhike, but you get to knock off two challenging birds and get a lot of free vertical with one climb (plus a little extra). If you wait too long in the season, you'd better have really sharp edges, because the couloir is known as one of the classic alpine ice climbs in the range.

During big snow years, there is a challenging alternative to Dana Couloir known as Solstice Couloir. Look for the corniced entry on the east edge of the peak before you reach the summit. For skiers looking for even more

East Chutes of Mount Dana.

challenge, the very steep Cocaine and Ripper chutes drop off the eastern edge of Dana Plateau, just south of the top of the Third Pillar. These gullies end up far down in Lee Vining Canyon, making for a total descent of nearly 7,000 feet. Ellery Bowl and the hidden Ellery Couloirs lie at the north end of the plateau. This option gives you about 4,500-feet of steep sliding fun. Of course, you don't have to go for the extreme. It is still very worthwhile to return the way you came, down the moderate north side of the peak.

Route: To reach the trailhead, turn west onto California 120 off US Highway 395 just south of the town of Lee Vining and climb 14 miles up Lee Vining Canyon. Park at the entrance to Yosemite National Park at Tioga Pass (9,945'), and follow the route of the summer trail up the north slopes of Mount Dana to the summit (13,057'). To reach the top of east-facing Dana Couloir, ski down the south side of the peak to the prominent saddle. The descent begins moderately, then gets steeper for an unrelieved 1,000-foot drop onto the glacier. Below the bergschrund, the angle relents, providing a fun run down Glacier Canyon past Dana Lake (11,100') to the slopes above the trailhead. Contour around to the west until you reach your car.

If you are planning to combine this descent with one of the Ellery Chutes, climb onto the bench above Dana Lake to reach the flat and rocky Dana Plateau. A prominent spur ridge divides Ellery Bowl from the east side descents. A very large cornice often blocks the entry into these descents. The easiest access is on the extreme eastern edge of the lip. A variety of very steep couloirs break through the cliffs on the left side of the plateau edge. These descents are discussed elsewhere. Pick your poison.

Dana Couloir, Mount Dana.

51 Ellery Bowl (11,582')

Route: Chute Out Couloir
Trailhead: Ellery Lake
Vertical: About 2,100'
Length: A few hours
Difficulty: Class 4-5
USGS 7.5' Maps: Mount Dana

Overview: Ellery Bowl offers perhaps the best roadside skiing in the entire range. As with neighboring Dana Couloir, this is a classic springtime ritual and can be a bit crowded. The best time to hit Ellery Bowl is just after the road opens, when good snow leads all the way back to the car. A large rock in the middle of the bowl makes for a convenient meeting place or lunch spot for groups of varying abilities. The run down to the car is quite moderate, while the steep stuff lies directly above the rock. The easiest route to the Dana Plateau is up the obvious slope on the left below a large cornice. On the descent, be aware that there is a large cliff on skier's left of the bowl.

The main attraction in Ellery Bowl is the central couloir, which became known as The Chute Out. This photogenic gully is lined by vertical rock walls. Like other couloirs dropping from the Dana Plateau, The Chute Out is often blocked on top by a large cornice, which is a very serious hazard, particularly later in the season. Many skiers have been hit by truck-sized

Ellery Chutes.

Stephen Pope skiing The Chute Out, Ellery Bowl.

blocks when the cornices above them fail. The three couloirs to your right are The Banana Chute, The S-Couloir, and The Poop Chute. These couloirs are similar to The Chute Out but not quite as aesthetic.

Route: To reach Ellery Lake, turn onto California 120 from US Highway 395 just south of the town of Lee Vining and head west for about 10 miles. Just past the ranger station, there is a good view of the chutes dropping off the east edge of the Dana Plateau, including the Cocaine and Ripper chutes and the prominent granite spire known as The Third Pillar. You can see the ice climbs of Lee Vining Canyon briefly as you make your way up the road, and, after crossing the Warren Fork of Lee Vining Creek, you can see Ellery Bowl. Park at the dam (9,500') and head uphill to the plateau (11,600') toward your chosen objective. The easiest route is the ascent bowl, while The Chute Out is the one to tick.

Some of the wildest ski descents in the Sierra are on the east side of the plateau. A series of extremely steep chutes drops between the towering granite pillars and into two great glacial cirques, then the terrain is very rugged terrain all the way down to Lee Vining Campground (7,400'). If you decide to ski one of the chutes on the east side, you'll need to leave a car at the campground or hitchhike back.

52 False White Mountain (12,002')

Route:	East face
Trailhead:	Tioga Pass Resort
Vertical:	About 2,600'
Length:	A few hours
Difficulty:	Class 3
USGS 7.5' Maps:	Tioga Pass, Mount Dana

Overview: In early spring, a great thing happens. Before they open California 120 all the way through Yosemite National Park, they clear the road for

East side of False White Mountain and White Mountain.

fishermen and skiers to the Tioga Pass Resort. In the winter, this backcountry resort is open for business and offers nearly unlimited access to excellent skiing. Be aware, though, that getting to the resort in the winter can sometimes involve serious avalanche hazard. The first runs north of Tioga Pass are short runs off the summit of Gaylor Peak. These are popular for repeat shots in the spring. The next peak west is the great east-facing bowl of False White Mountain. This surprisingly moderate descent is one of the most popular in the range. Nearby Tioga Peak also offers a number of excellent descents directly above the resort.

Route: You can access False White Mountain from Gaylor Peak, Tioga Pass Resort, or the Saddlebag Road at Sawmill Campground (9,400'). The first approach follows the crest west to the summit. The second ascends past the ruins of the historic mining town of Bennettville and onto Fantail Lake (9,950'). The Fantail Gullies lie just above. The route from Sawmill meets this one at Spuller Lake (10,300') before climbing a broad gully to the south and accessing the bowl below the north summit (12,002'). The south summit is higher and offers steeper skiing. Another great place for bowl skiing in this area is the ridge (11,200') just south of Saddlebag Lake (10,100'). There is a wide variety of slopes and gullies towards Mount Conness, as well as the excellent north couloir above broad Conness Glacier. Finally, as noted above, Tioga Peak (11,513') offers many fine runs on its south side in early season and on the north side later in the year.

53 North Peak (12,242')

Route:	North couloirs
Trailhead:	Tioga Pass Resort
Vertical:	About 2,700'
Length:	Half day
Difficulty:	Class 4-5
USGS 7.5' Maps:	Tioga Pass, Mount Dana

Overview: The north face of North Peak is very sheer and split by a trio of very steep couloirs. The main shot is the westernmost gully. This leads to an obvious notch below the summit ridge, while the other two couloirs do not reach all the way to the ridge. All of these couloirs are in excess of 45 degrees and cross a gaping bergschrund to reach the glacier. Later in the season, these routes become classic alpine ice climbs, and the ice is never too far below the surface, so sharpen your edges. These gullies have been the site of a number of accidents, and although they are reasonably close to the road, they are serious endeavors. However, for highly skilled skiers and boarders, these extreme runs are as good as you'll find anywhere.

North face of North Peak.

Route: North Peak is at the west end of Saddlebag Lake and is also known as the North Peak of Mount Conness. Access is via Tioga Pass Resort. To reach the resort, turn west onto California 120 from US Highway 395 just south of the town of Lee Vining and follow Tioga Pass Road for 14 miles up Lee Vining Canyon. Park at the turnoff to Saddlebag Lake near Tioga Pass Resort (9,500') and follow the road up to Saddlebag Lake (10,100'). Cross the lake and head toward scenic Twenty Lakes Basin at the base of pointed North Peak. Climb onto the glacier at the base of the peak (11,000') and pick your chute. If these choices are too steep, the southeast slopes are more moderate and offer a great descent from the summit (12,242').

54   Excelsior Mountain (12,446')

Route: Burro Creek
Trailheads: Virginia Lakes and Lundy Lake
Vertical: About 4,500'
Length: All day
Difficulty: Class 3-4
USGS 7.5' Maps: Dunderberg Peak

Overview: The descent of Excelsior Mountain is relatively unique in the Sierra. Due to the high trailhead in Virginia Lakes, you can make a relatively short tour to the summit and then a fairly good-sized descent into

East side of Excelsior Mountain.

adjacent Lundy Canyon. It is easy to get lost when navigating the descent, though, because the peak is very large and drains into four major canyons on its east flank alone—Green, Virginia, Lundy, and Lee Vining canyons. In addition, the lower reaches of the peak harbor very impressive cliffs, so if you don't follow the right-hand route, you could end up on top of a waterfall with a horrendous climb back out, or worse. This peak has been the site of some bad accidents. However, if you've got your stuff together, this is a great trip.

Route: The tour begins at Virginia Lakes (9,700'). To reach the trailhead, turn west off US Highway 395 at Conway Summit and drive to the end of the plowed road. There's plenty here to distract you from your tour. The impressive gullies of Dunderberg Peak (12,374') lie to the north, while the excellent bowls of Mount Olsen (11,086'), South Peak (11,300'), and Black Mountain (11,797') lie to the south directly above the lakes. To reach Excelsior Mountain, follow the drainage up past Blue Lake (9,900') and on to Frog Lakes (10,375'). Then, follow the general course of the summer trail to the low saddle (11,150') to the west. Stay on the ridgeline and head southwest to reach the summit ridge of Excelsior Mountain (12,446'). The peak has four summits, basically at the head of each canyon. The tallest is in the middle, directly above Lundy Canyon.

From the main summit, head northeast down a moderately steep slope onto a small glacier and continue east down this drainage to Burro Lake (10,500'). From the lake, the drainage turns southeast, begins to drop more steeply, and enters Lundy Canyon. Stay to the right (south of the creek) until you reach the treeline, then head out along the canyon floor to reach the parking area at the lake (7,760').

55 South Peak (11,400')

Route: East chutes

Trailhead: Virginia Lakes

Vertical: About 2,200'

Length: A few hours

Difficulty: Class 3

USGS 7.5' Maps: Dunderberg Peak

Overview: As previously noted, the entire Viginia Lakes area offers a wealth of wonderful ski descents. Of particular interest, however, are the twin chutes dropping from the summit of South Peak. These chutes, clearly visible from US Highway 395 in the vicinity of Conway Summit, are well worth the detour. Other worthwhile ventures in the area include the north shoulder of Mount Olsen, which offers good open tree skiing, and the northeast bowl of Black Mountain, which drops down to the end of the road at Red Lake. Obviously, the slopes of Dunderberg Peak across the canyon are worthy, too.

Route: To reach the trailhead, leave US Highway 395 at the top of Conway Summit and drive west on Virginia Lakes Road until you reach the summer cabins (9,700'). Early in the season, the road may not be plowed, so you will have to ski a few extra miles to access the peak. From the cabins, turn south and climb the gullies or the shallow ridge between them to reach the summit (11,400'). If you are interested in Black Mountain, continue up the road to Red Lake; then ascend the bowl to the east of the summit (11,760').

East face of South Peak.

56 Dunderberg Peak (12,374')

Route:	Southeast bowl
Trailhead:	Virginia Lakes
Vertical:	About 2,700'
Length:	A few hours
Difficulty:	Class 3
USGS 7.5' Maps:	Dunderberg Peak

Overview: Dunderberg Peak is another mountain that has great ski descents on all sides. The north side has a number of moderately steep bowls leading down from the twin summits to Dunderberg Creek and the four-wheel-drive road from Virginia Lakes. The north bowl between the summits is especially fun. A very steep couloir leads off the north side of the taller west summit. A fine couloir drops almost straight down to Virginia Lakes from the saddle between the two summits. However, the southeast bowl leading from the east summit to the summer cabins is the finest and most popular descent on the peak. In addition, the entire Viginia Lakes area offers a wealth of wonderful ski descents. The bowls across the canyon on Black Mountain and South Peak are especially worthy of attention.

Route: To reach the trailhead, leave US Highway 395 at the top of Conway Summit and drive west on Virginia Lakes Road until you reach the summer cabins (9,700'). Early in the season, the road may not be plowed and you will have to ski a few extra miles to access the peak. From the cabins, follow

Southeast bowl, Dunderberg Peak.

the obvious avalanche path north to reach the broad southeast bowl of the peak. Stick to the eastern edge of the bowl and gain the summit ridge well to the east of the summit (12,374'). This provides the easiest ascent, as well as the most moderate descent. Follow the ridgeline west to reach the east summit of the peak. Depending on conditions, you may want to drop in right off the summit or pick a more southerly aspect for better corn. The gentle terrain at the bottom of the bowl is perfect for laying out some high speed giant slalom arcs. Have fun!

57 Twin Peaks (12,240')

Route: North couloir
Trailhead: Twin Lakes
Vertical: About 5,100'
Length: All day
Difficulty: Class 4
USGS 7.5' Maps: Matterhorn Peak, Dunderberg Peak, Buckeye Ridge

Overview: The little known Twin Peaks is protected by a lack of visibility from the usual viewpoints, as well as by a much more famous neighbor. Sierra skiers have long considered the east couloir of Matterhorn Peak to be one of the classics of the range, yet Twin Peaks offers three gullies that are

North face of Twin Peaks.

Late spring powder on Twin Peaks.

equal to Matterhorn Peak in length, pitch, and quality. If you know where to look, you can catch a glimpse of these gullies briefly when driving south on US Highway 395. Just south of Devils Gate, the road makes a turn and empties out into an open field. Twin Peaks is on the skyline to the southwest and the three gullies are in plain sight, one between the twin summits and twin gullies on the east ridge. Then they are quickly hidden by the bulk of Crater Crest. If you can get a copy of H.J. Burhenne's *Sierra Spring Ski Touring* (long out of print), there is a great picture of the peak taken from nearby Crater Crest. If that's not enough, go up there and have a look for yourself.

Route: Turn south off US Highway 395 onto Twin Lakes Road at the town of Bridgeport and continue to the trailhead at Mono Village Campground on the west end of the lakes (7,100'). Leave the campground, cross Robinson Creek on a bridge, and take the trail up Horse Creek to upper Horse Creek Meadow. Follow this broad canyon all the way up the glacier below the peak. The steep central couloir of Twin Peaks (12,323') is just ahead above the gaping bergschrund. There is another glacier with twin gullies rising up to the ridge of the east summit across the low ridge. Any of these routes is worth the effort. Of course, the run back down Horse Creek is justly considered to be one of the best in the range.

58 Matterhorn Peak (12,264')

Route:	East couloir
Trailhead:	Twin Lakes
Vertical:	About 5,100'
Length:	All day
Difficulty:	Class 4
USGS 7.5' Maps:	Matterhorn Peak, Dunderberg Peak, Buckeye Ridge

Overview: The east couloir of Matterhorn Peak has long been a goal of many Sierra ski mountaineers. Lying in the shadow of the great north prow of the peak, this steep couloir drops straight onto the glacier. People have been skiing Matterhorn Peak for decades, and this gully is certain to catch the eye of any skier traveling through Bridgeport during the winter or spring. The gully is also classic because the steepest part is in the middle. Once past the cornice that may guard the entrance to the couloir, the angle eases a bit, allowing you to get your rhythm.

North side of Matterhorn Peak.

Matterhorn Peak

1

West
Couloir

East
Couloir

Ski
Dreams

East couloir of Matterhorn Peak.

As you continue, however, the gully bulges and gets dramatically steeper before finally mellowing out again at the glacier. This is followed by the great run back down Horse Creek to Twin Lakes. There are a number of other gullies in the area worth trying, including the obvious Ski Dreams route to the east of the peak.

Route: To reach the trailhead at Twin Lakes, turn south off US Highway 395 onto Twin Lakes Road in the town of Bridgeport and continue to the trailhead at Mono Village Campground (7,100'). From the parking area, cross Robinson Creek on the bridge at the entrance to the campground and take the trail up into Horse Creek. The trail disappears in the hanging valley of the creek, but the drainage is easy to follow. Near the head, cut west and ascend a moderately steep slope to reach the glacier (11,000'). The couloir is very obvious from the glacier. At the top of the couloir, the summit (12,264') is a short scramble away. Think twice before committing to the long, steep descent. The west couloir is about the same in terms of challenge. The run down Horse Creek is just good, clean fun. Depending on the snow line, you may be able to ski all the way back to the lake.

59 Mount Walt (11,581')

Route:	Burhenne Couloir
Trailhead:	Twin Lakes
Vertical:	About 4,500'
Length:	Half day
Difficulty:	Class 3-4
USGS 7.5' Maps:	Matterhorn Peak, Buckeye Ridge

Overview: Mount Walt is an interesting peak. You won't find the peak's name on any maps, and it has been called many names over the years. In his book *Sierra Spring Ski Touring*, H.J. Burhenne listed this peak as one of the classics and named the peak in honor of his frequent companion, Walter Herbert. Now Mr. Burhenne is gone, too. On maps, you will find this peak as the northern of the two peaks listed as 11,581 feet on the ridge between Little Slide and Blacksmith canyons. In fact, both peaks offer good skiing and are quite obvious from Mono Village at the west end of Twin Lakes. They form the apparent northern terminus of jagged Sawtooth Ridge. The broad snowslope of the southern

East side of Mount Walt.

peak is Eocene Peak, while the pointy one to the north is Mount Walt. Climbers know Mount Walt as the actual summit located well above the rock tower of The Incredible Hulk in Little Slide Canyon.

Route: To reach the trailhead at Twin Lakes, turn south off US Highway 395 onto Twin Lakes Road in the town of Bridgeport and continue past the west end of the lakes to the trailhead at Mono Village Campground (7,100'). Head west through the campground and follow Robinson Creek to the edge of the campground. A bridge crosses the creek at the site of a private fish hatchery. Climb the steep slope above to reach the confluence of the two forks of Blacksmith Creek (8,100'). Take the right fork and follow it until you can climb the western wall of the canyon to a saddle (10,200') north of the peak. This stretch is fairly steep. Turn south and follow the ridge to the narrow summit (11,581'). Enjoy the view of the many fine granite spires in the area before heading back down. Don't forget to think of the pioneer ski mountaineers like Herbert and Burhenne who used three-foot firn gliders on peaks like this.

60 Crater Crest (11,394')

Route:	North gullies
Trailhead:	Twin Lakes
Vertical:	About 4,100'
Length:	A few hours
Difficulty:	Class 3
USGS 7.5' Maps:	Matterhorn Peak, Buckeye Ridge

North side of Crater Crest.

Overview: Crater Crest is a great ski peak that has little attraction for mountaineers. The north gullies drop dramatically into the waters of Twin Lakes and are major-league avalanche terrain. This was another favorite peak of the Tahoe ski mountaineers in the 1960s, and rightly so. Depending on your mood, you can take a steeper line down the central gully or a more moderate descent on the side. Any way you go, Crater Crest is good fun and a worthwhile peak descent.

Route: To reach the trailhead at Twin Lakes, turn south off US Highway 395 onto Twin Lakes Road in the town of Bridgeport and continue past the east end of the lakes (7,100'). Climb onto the east ridge and follow this to the summit (11,394'). From here, you have a number of choices for the descent to the lakes. All the options are equally good and equally scary in periods of high avalanche hazard. Be careful.

APPENDIX: Wilderness Permits and Information

Wilderness permits are required for overnight travel in all designated wilderness, primitive, and national park backcountry areas. Quotas are if effect for the most popular overnight areas, beginning in late spring. Prior to the quota period, wilderness permits are available at the locations listed below. Day use is not currently regulated, except for Mount Whitney. Wilderness permits are made available on March 1 for the following summer. If all of the advance permits have been issued, you will need to apply for your permit in person on the date you wish to enter the wilderness. These permits are available at trailhead kiosks or at the local ranger stations. Contact the listed agencies well in advance. They will advise you on daily quotas, wood fires, area closures, and other regulations concerning wilderness travel.

Inyo National Forest
Mammoth Ranger District
Highway 203, P.O. Box 148
Mammoth Lakes, CA 93546
760-924-5500

Inyo National Forest
Mono Lake Ranger District
P.O. Box 429
Lee Vining, CA 93541
760-647-3044

Inyo National Forest
Mount Whitney Ranger District
P.O. Box 8, South Highway 395
Lone Pine, CA 93545
760-876-6200

Inyo National Forest
White Mountain Ranger District
798 North Main Street
Bishop, CA 93514
760-873-2500

Sequoia and Kings Canyon
    National Parks
47050 Generals Highway
Three Rivers, CA 93271
209-565-3341

Sierra National Forest
Pineridge Ranger District
P.O. Box 559
Prather, CA 93651
209-855-5355

Sierra National Forest
Mariposa-Minarets Ranger
    District
P.O. Box 10
North Fork, CA 93643
209-877-2218

Toiyabe National Forest
Bridgeport Ranger District
P.O. Box 595
Bridgeport, CA 93516
760-932-7070

Yosemite National Park
P.O. Box 577
Yosemite, CA 95389
209-372-0265

Index

ABOUT THE AUTHOR

John Moynier has been guiding folks on backcountry tours and descents in the Sierra for nearly twenty years. He is a certified ski mountaineering guide with the American Mountain Guides Association (AMGA) and serves as clinician and examiner for their ski mountaineering program. He is also a professional member of the American Association of Avalanche Professionals (AAAP) and works as a backcountry avalanche forecaster for the eastern Sierra region. Check out his daily bulletins at www.csac.org. In addition, John is fully certified as an alpine, snowboard, telemark, Nordic, and backcountry instructor by the Professional Ski

John Moynier.

Instructors of America-West (PSIA-W) and has been an examiner and clinician for these disciplines for many years.

John is also a freelance writer and photographer, with frequent contributions in many outdoor publications, including *Backcountry; Powder, Rock and Ice; Climbing;* and *Shutterbug.* He has also been an editor with *Couloir* and *Cross Country Skier,* and he has written a number of books, including *Sierra Classics, Avalanche Aware; Mammoth Area Rock Climbs; Bishop Area Rock Climbs; The Basic Essentials of Cross Country Skiing;* and *The Basic Essentials of Mountaineering.* John lives in Bishop, California, with his wife Rose, daughter Katie, and their snow-loving doggies.